Sacred Mushrooms & the Law

Sacred Mushrooms & the Law

by Richard Glen Boire, ESQ.

Ronin Publishing

Berkeley, CA

Sacred Mushrooms & The Law

ISBN: 978-157951-061-9

Published by
RONIN Publishing, Inc.
PO Box 3436
Oakland CA, 94609
roninpub.com

Credits:

Editor:	Beverly A. Potter docpotter.com
Cover Design:	Judy July, Generic Type generictype.com
Fonts:	Meso Deko by Deniart Systems Maya Day Names by Deniart Systems Chisel EF by Elsner Flake Design Studios Benguiat Goudy Old Style

Distributed to the trade by **Publishers Group West**
Printed in the United States of America
Library of Congress Card Number: 2002109578

There is a world beyond ours,
A world that is far away, nearby, and invisible.
And there is where God lives,
Where the dead live, the spirits and the saints,
A world where everything has already happened
And everything is known.

—María Sabina

Notice to Reader:

MANUFACTURING OUTLAWED DRUGS and possessing outlawed drugs or plants is a crime that can result in a lengthy term of imprisonment and significant fines. This publication is offered for educational purposes and is not meant to encourage any illicit activities. The Publisher and Author assume no liability for your actions and caution you to seek legal advice from a competent, accredited attorney. The information provided herein is subject to change without notice and is not intended to be, nor should it be considered, a substitute for individualized legal advice rendered by a competent attorney.

Table of Contents

Forward by Terence McKenna 9
Introduction 11
1. Cognitive Liberty 14
2. The First Amendment 20
3. Federal Law 25
4. State Law 35
5. Spores & Growing Kits 38
Part II Court Decisions
6. The Allen Case 49
7. The Fiske Case 51
8. The Dunlap Case 54
9. The Patterson Case 58
10. The Justice Case 61
11. The Wohlever Case 63
12. The Kail Case 65
13. The Bemis Case 67
14. The Ryan Case 72
15. The Atley Case 74
16. Canadian Cases 84
Part III Defenses
17. Substance versus Mushroom Defense 89
18. Religious Defense 95
Part IV Political Implications
19. Taxonomy 101
20. Legal Harm Reduction 104
Bibliography 115
Alchemind Society 117
Ronin Books 120

Foreword

by Terence McKenna

"The Law is an Ass," observed Charles Dickens, when reflecting on the child labor laws in 19th century England. His observation is even more cogent when applied to the present day legal approach to psychedelic and psychoactive plants by the high tech, industrial pseudo-democracies, especially the United States.

This manual on the current legal status of psilocybin/psilocin provides valuable information to anyone caught in the Kafkaesque *danse macabre* of "preparing their defense." As for the rest of us, psychedelic activists and students of the grotesque underbelly of American justice, we can only marvel at the moronic response of a judicial system only too eager to blur distinctions and trample rights in its hurry to discredit and extinguish forms of religious expression outside the "Christian Family" of tired name brand cults.

In the Middle Ages this approach led to the trying of domestic animals for capital crimes in which they might have been involved. Today, in what are supposedly some of the most socially advanced societies in the world, the constipated judicial mind has no difficulty in dishing up equally absurd prosecutions, many examples of which will be found in *Sacred Mushrooms & the Law*.

The fact is that the Western Mind is profoundly uneasy in the presence of forms of inebriation and religious expression with which it is unfamiliar. *Sacred Mushrooms & the Law* shows how quickly this unease is transformed into persecution and the erosion of everyone's rights of free expression and freedom of religion.

I am happy to call attention to this fine little work in the hope that the continued folly of psychedelic plant and substance persecution, which is but the tip of an iceberg of larger social decay and contradiction, will soon give way to a more enlightened approach—an approach which deeper thinkers on American drug policy have long known was inevitable.

—TERENCE MCKENNA

Introduction

WHILE VISIONARY MUSHROOMS exist in a fairly wide range of genera, this book focuses on the law pertaining to those mushrooms and their endogenously produced psychoactive constituents which have most successfully permeated our culture. Carl Ruck and his group of schlars proposed the word "entheogen" for such psychoactive plants.

Most of the detailed information herein pertains to the substances psilocybin and psilocin, which have been confirmed in over 80 different species of mushrooms, most of which are within the genus *Psilocybe.* In this book, you will learn how the U.S. legal system has dealt with sacred mushrooms and fungophiles who possess or grow them. You will learn the few bright-line rules that exist, and explore the many gray areas of the law. As with the mushrooms themselves, you will find that much of mushroom law is, itself, mysteries and all but incomprehensible.

This is a story of pushing and pulling, of shifting shapes unsteady landscapes, and the stiff legs of the law. Whereas the mushrooms dance on the hinterlands of our minds, offering us multiple escape routes through the thicket of cultural control, the law is always visible in the distance, its long arm stretched like Pinocchio's nose.

Substratus

THE MOMENT when humans discovered the visionary properties of *teonanácatl* or "sacred mushrooms" is lost in the substrates of history. Despite its untraceable genesis, knowledge of the magical properties of certain mushrooms has been passed from mind to mind and mouth to mouth, reaching us here on the unfolding edge of the present.

As in 1620 when the Holy Office of the Inquisition proclaimed the ingestion of all visionary plants a heresy, users of sacred mushrooms at the dawn of the 21st Century have also been marked as enemies of the State.

Soma

AMANITA MUSCARIA, is one of the oldest shamanic inebriants known. In fact, in *Soma, Divine Mushroons of Immortality* Wasson says that it may well be the sacred "Soma" discussed in the Hindu Vedas. *Amanita muscaria* and its close relative *Amanita pantherina* have been ingested for their vision-producing properties for thousands of years. Some people continue to use them today. Their primary psychoactive principle is ibotenic acid, which is not a controlled substance under federal or state law. The secondary principle, muscimol, is also unscheduled.

In 1958, working with *Psilocybe mexicana* mushrooms cultured from samples obtained from the now famous

Mazatec curandera María Sabina, Dr. Albert Hofmann isolated two indole derivatives that he named psilocybin (4-phosphoryloxy-N,N-dimethyltryptamine) and psilocin (4-hydroxy-N,N-dimethyltryptamine). By most accounts, psilocin is markedly more psychoactive than psilocybin. And, as nature would have it, inside the human body psilocybin is largely converted into psilocin.

ENTHEOGEN DEFINED

In Greek, the word entheos *means literally "god (theos) within," and was used to describe the condition that follows when one is inspired and possessed by the god that has entered one's body. It was applied to prophetic seizures, erotic passion and artistic creation, as well as to those religious rites in which mystical states were experienced through the ingestion of substances that were transubstantial with the deity. . . . with the Greek root* gen *(it) denotes the action of "becoming,"*

–Carl Ruck

Nature's Illicit Drug Labs

STAMETS REPORTS in *Psilocybin Mushrooms of the World* that dried *Psilocybe cubensis* mushrooms contain approximately 0.6 percent of both psilocybin and psilocin, meaning that every gram–1000 mgs–of dried *P. cubensis* contains about 12 milligrams of psilocybin and psilocin. Both Stamets and Ott report that effects that might be considered "entheogenic" begin around 20 milligrams psilocybin/psilocin–or approximately two grams of dried *P. cubensis*–for a person weighing approximately 150 pounds. A strong dose would be approximately 50 milligrams psilocybin/psilocin, or about five grams dried *Psilocybe cubensis.*

1

Cognitive Liberty

WORDS ARE CARRIERS of thoughts, whether spoken from mouth to ear, digitized and passed electronically, or downloaded into ink and passed on paper across time and space. As you read this sentence you are receiving information. Because words are vehicles for thoughts, words can change your opinion, give you new ideas, reform your worldview, or foment a revolution.

Attempts to control the written word date from at least AD 325 when the Council of Nicaea ruled that Christ was 100 percent divine and forbade the dissemination of contrary beliefs. Since the invention of the printing press in 1452, governments have struggled to control the printed word. Presses were initially licensed and registered. Only certain people were permitted to own or control a printing press and only certain things could be printed or copied. This was the origin of today's copyright rules, by the way. Works printed without prior authorization were gathered up and destroyed and the authors and printers were imprisoned.

Scholars disagree as to the exact date, but some time around 1560, Pope Paul IV published the *Index Librorum Prohibitorum*, which was a list of forbidden books–i.e., controlled substances–enforced by the Roman government. When the *Index* was–finally–abandoned in 1966, it listed over 4,000 forbidden books, including works by Galileo, Kant, Pascal, Spinoza and John Locke. The history of censorship has been extensively recorded by others. The point is simply the obvious one that efforts to prohibit heterodox texts and to make criminals out of those who "manufactured" such texts, were not so much interested in controlling ink patterns on paper, as in controlling the *ideas* encoded in printed words.

> **...without freedom of thought there can be no free society.**
>
> – U.S. Supreme Court Justice Felix Frankfurter

I submit that in the same way, the so-called "war-on-drugs" is not a war on pills, powder, plants, and potions, it is war on mental states. It is a war on consciousness itself–how much, what sort we are permitted to experience, and who gets to control it. More than an unintentional misnomer, the government-termed "war on drugs" is a strategic decoy label; a slight-of-hand move by the government to redirect attention away from what lies at ground zero of the war–each individual's fundamental right to control his or her own consciousness.

Drug War Newspeak

IN GEORGE ORWELL'S dystopian novel *Nineteen Eighty-Four*, the Oceania government diligently worked to establish "Newspeak" a carefully crafted language designed by the government for the purpose of making unapproved "modes of thought impossible." Prior to Newspeak, the people of Oceania communicated in "Oldspeak," an autonomous natural language capable of expressing nuances of emotion and multiple points of view. By controlling language through the imposition of Newspeak–by eliminating undesirable words–the government of Oceania was able to control and, in some cases, completely extinguish certain thoughts.

A character in *Nineteen Eighty-Four* explained to Winston Smith, "Don't you see that the whole aim of Newspeak is to narrow the range of thought?...Every year there are fewer and fewer words, and the range of consciousness is always a little smaller." People raised with Newspeak, having never known the wider-range of Oldspeak, might fail to notice, indeed, might be unable to even perceive, that the Government was limiting consciousness.

In 1970, just four years after the Catholic Church finally abandoned the *Index Librorum Prohibitorum*, the United States government produced its own index of forbidden thought-catalysts–the federal schedule of controlled substances. Included on the initial list of Schedule I substances were seventeen substances denoted as "hallucinogens," which were declared to have "a high potential for abuse," "no currently accepted medical use," and "a lack of accepted safety" even under medical supervision. Among the list of outlawed hallucinogens were psilocybin and psilocin, the active principles of *Psilocybe* mushrooms. The experience elicited by these substances in their chemical and natural fungi forms is the *par excellence* of Oldspeak–a cognitive modality dating from pre-history.

Mushrooms, of the genus *Psilocybe*, were used to occasion visionary states at least as early as 4000 B.C. The *Psilocybe* mushroom was used in religious ceremonies long before the Aztec civilization. Some who ingest visionary mushrooms believe that the mushrooms talk to them and open up channels of communication with animals and other entities. As Henry Munn reported, Mazatec eaters of *Psilocybe* mushrooms are adamant that the mushrooms speak to them:

> "The Mazatecs say that the mushrooms speak. If you ask a shaman where his imagery comes from, he is likely to reply: "I didn't say it, the mushrooms did." ...he who eats these mushrooms, if he is a man of language, becomes endowed with an inspired capacity to speak.... The spontaneity they liberate is not only perceptual, but linguistic, the spontaneity of speech, of fervent, lucid discourse, of the logos in activity. For the shaman it is as if existence were uttering itself through him...words are materializations of consciousness; language is a privileged vehicle of our relation to reality."

Just as Newspeak was intended to make certain Old(speak) thoughts literally unthinkable, so the War-on-Entheogens makes certain sorts of cognition and awareness all but inaccessible. Religious scholar Peter Lamborn Wilson has aptly framed the War-on-Entheogens as a battle over the nature of thought itself:

> "The War-on-Drugs is a war on cognition itself, about thought itself as the human condition. Is thought this dualist Cartesian reason? Or is cognition this mysterious, complex, organic, magical thing with little mushroom elves dancing around. Which is it to be?"

In Orwell's vision of *1984*, Newspeak's power to control and limit thought depended, in part, upon the passing of time and the birth of new generations that never knew Oldspeak. As explained by Orwell in the Appendix to *Nineteen Eighty-Four*,

> "It was intended that when Newspeak had been adopted once and for all and Oldspeak forgotten, a heretical thought–that is a thought diverging from the principles of Ingsoc–should be literally unthinkable, at least so far as thought is dependant on words."

Much as Newspeak depended in part upon time-eradicating knowledge of Oldspeak, today's War-on-Entheogens is sustainable, in part, because the current generation of young adults–21-30 year olds–have never known a time when most entheogens were not illegal. Those who have never experienced the mental states that are now prohibited do not realize what the laws are denying them. It is as if nothing is being taken away, at least nothing noticeable, nothing that is missed. As pointed out by Arons and Lawrence, authors of a law review article on how mandatory schooling raises issues of mass-consciousness control: "the more the government regulates formation of beliefs so as to interfere with personal consciousness,...the fewer people can conceive dissenting ideas or perceive contradictions between self-interest and government sustained ideological orthodoxy."

Because of the personal experiential nature of mushroom-occasioned cognition, only those who have been initiated into the modern day Mysteries—those who have tasted the forbidden fruit from the visionary fungi of knowledge and have not fallen victim to the stigmatizing psycho-impact of "being a drug user"—are acutely aware of the gravity of what is being prohibited; powerful modalities for thinking, perceiving, and experiencing.

The very best argument for the potential value of the mushroomed state of mind is in the entheogenic experience itself—an experience that has, for all practical purposes been outlawed. This is the dilemma of entheogen policy reformation. The advocate for entheogenic consciousness is left in an even worse position than the proverbial sighted man who must describe colors to a blind person. With regard to entheogen policy, the position is worse because the "blind" are in power and have declared it a crime to see colors.

We are being denied powerful modalities for thinking, perceiving and experiencing.

Left with the impossible task of saying the unsayable, of describing the indescribable, those who have tasted the forbidden fungi are left to plead their case on the fundamental philosophical and political level of what it means to be truly free. They must state their appeal on the ground that, with respect to the inner-workings of each person's mind, the values of tolerance and respect are far weightier and far more conducive to the basic principles of democracy, than is the chillingly named "zero-tolerance" policy that is currently in vogue. This brings us, once again, to cognitive liberty as an essential substrate of freedom.

2

The First Amendment

BENJAMIN CARDOZO, one of the most respected and influential American legal scholars of the 20th Century and a former Justice of the U.S. Supreme Court, affirmed cognitive liberty as central to most every other freedom:

> ...freedom of thought...one may say...is the matrix, the indispensable condition, of nearly every other form of freedom. With rare aberrations a pervasive recognition of that truth can be traced in our history, political and legal. (*Palko v. Connecticut* (1937) 302 U.S. 319, 326-327.)

The First Amendment's guarantees were designed to bar the government from controlling or prohibiting the dissemination of unpopular or dissenting ideas. Central to all five guarantees is the

> **THE FIRST AMENDMENT**
>
> *Congress shall make no law respecting an establishment of religion, or prohibiting the free exercise thereof; or abridging the freedom of speech, or of the press; or the right of the people peaceably to assemble, and to petition the Government for a redress of grievances.*

acknowledgement that people must be treated by the government as ends not means. Each person must be free to develop his or her own belief system and to express his or her thoughts in the so-called "marketplace of ideas." As U.S. Supreme Court Justice Felix Frankfurter emphasized in 1949, the freedom of expression guaranteed by the First Amendment guards against "thought becom[ing] checked and atrophied."

Free speech, free exercise, free association, a free press and the right to assemble are all moot if the thought that underlies these actions has already been constrained by the government. If the government is permitted to prohibit the experiencing of certain thought processes, or otherwise manipulate consciousness at its very roots–via drug prohibitions, religious indoctrination, monopolizing media, or any number of methods–it need never worry about controlling the expression of such thoughts. By prohibiting the very formation of mind states–by stifling the free mind itself–free expression is made meaningless.

Thus, in order to prevent the erosion of the First Amendment's protection of expression, the Amendment must also provide at least as strong a protection for the underlying consciousness that forms the ideas that are later expressed. Indeed, the First Amendment is infused with the principle that each individual–not the government–ought to have control over his or her own mind to think what he or she wants to think and to freely form and express opinions and beliefs based on all the information at his or her disposal. The First Amendment, in other words, embraces cognitive liberty intwo ways. first, as the desired outcome of the articulated guarantees. Second, as a necessary precondition to those guaranteed freedoms.

By prohibiting the very formation of mind states–by stifling the free mind itself–free expression is made meaningless.

It's *My* Consciousness

In the apropos year of 1984, the Tenth Circuit Court of Appeal issued an opinion in a case involving a man who was involuntarily drugged with the anti-psychotic drug thorazine while he was being held for trial on murder charges. (*Bee v. Greaves* (10th Cir. 1984) 744 F.2d 1387, 1393.

The threshold issue was whether pretrial detainees have a fundamental right to refuse treatment with anti-psychotic drugs. To answer this question, the Tenth Circuit analogized to a 1982 case in which the U.S. Supreme Court held that "'[l]iberty from bodily restraint always has been recognized as the core of the liberty protected by the Due Process Clause from arbitrary governmental action.'" (*Youngberg v. Romeo* (1982) 457 U.S. 307, 316.) The Tenth Circuit reasoned that if freedom from *bodily* restraints is a fundamental right, then individuals must also have a liberty interest in freedom from "mental restraint of the kind potentially imposed by anti-psychotic drugs."

Thus, the Tenth Circuit found that freedom from government-imposed mental restraints was just as fundamental as freedom from government-imposed physical restraints—both were protected by the Due Process Clause. Furthermore, the Tenth Circuit found that the First Amendment was also implicated when the government attempts to involuntarily psycho-medicate a person awaiting trial. In unequivocal language, the Tenth Circuit explained

> "[t]he First Amendment protects communication of ideas, which itself implies protection of the capacity to produce ideas."

Professor Laurence Tribe of Harvard Law School has cautioned

> "In a society whose 'whole constitutional heritage rebels at the thought of giving government the power to control men's own minds,' the governing institutions, and especially the courts, must not only reject direct attempts to exercise forbidden domination over mental processes; they must strictly examine as well oblique intrusions likely to produce or designed to produce, the same result."

Prohibiting an otherwise law-abiding person from using entheogens is more than merely an "oblique intrusion" on the right to control one's own mental processes, or a slight trespass on the "protected capacity to produce ideas"—it is a direct frontal attack. Under the *National Drug Control Strategy* 2000, the federal government allocated just shy of $20 billion–$20,000,000,000–on an all out attempt to keep people from evoking alternative states of consciousness by the use of controlled substances.

History has shown, however, that government attempts to control consciousness are ultimately futile. The edges are unmapped for good reason. Therein hide the mysterious mushrooms, and other plants of knowledge. And therein, glimpsed only by our peripheral vision, darts freedom and those who love it.

3

Federal Law

THE FIRST FEDERAL LAW to regulate psilocybin and psilocin was enacted in July of 1965, and went into effect on February 1, 1966. [Pub. L. No. 89-74, 79 Stat. 226 (1965)]. Known as the Drug Abuse Control Amendments of 1965 (DACA), it amended the federal Food, Drug and Cosmetic Act by prohibiting the unregistered possession, manufacture, or sale of depressant, stimulant and hallucinogenic drugs. DACA did not explicitly name the proscribed "hallucinogenic" substances. Rather, it broadly and vaguely brought within its ambit any drug said to have a "hallucinogenic effect on the central nervous system."

While the DACA outlawed the possession of all hallucinogenic substances, an accompanying provision carved out a large exception. The exception permitted people to possess such drugs so long as they were for the personal use of the possessor, a member of his household, or for administration to an animal.

Criminalization

POSSESSION OF PSILOCYBIN and psilocin, even for personal use, became a Federal crime on October 24, 1968. [Pub.L. No. 90-639, 82 Stat. 1361 (1968)]. A first conviction for possessing either substance was punishable by a maximum of one year imprisonment and a $1,000 fine. A conviction for manufacturing or selling–or possessing with intent to sell–psilocin or psilocybin was punishable by a maximum of five years imprisonment and a $10,000 fine.

Controlled Substances Act

IN 1970, Congress enacted the Comprehensive Drug Abuse Prevention and Control Act of 1970, which became effective on October 27 of that year. Part II of this Act, known as the Controlled Substances Act (CSA), [21 U.S.C. Sec. 801 et. seq.] established a scheduling scheme whereby selected substances were grouped according to a checklist that rated each substance's addiction or abuse potential, medical efficacy, and medical safety.

Both psilocybin and psilocin were summarily declared to have "a high potential for abuse," "no currently accepted medical use" in the USA, and "a lack of accepted safety," even under medical supervision. They were thereupon placed in Schedule I–the most restrictive schedule–and denoted "hallucinogens." The substances were assigned the DEA controlled substance code numbers 7437 (psilocybin) and 7438 (psilocin).

Under the CSA, "any material, compound, mixture, or preparation, which contains any quantity of [psilocybin or psilocin], or which contains any of their salts, isomers, or salts of isomers" is also considered a Schedule I controlled substance.

Federal Crimes

TODAY, the CSA remains the principal federal law criminalizing a host of actions involving psilocybin and psilocin. Under federal law, even *attempting* to possess, manufacture, or import/export psilocybin or psilocin is a crime. It is punished the same as if the offenses were successfully committed. (21 U.S.C. sec. 846.)

Under the CSA it is also a federal crime to:

(1) Knowingly or intentionally possess psilocybin or psilocin.

(2) Manufacture, distribute, or dispense psilocybin or psilocin, or possess either substance with the intent to manufacture, distribute or dispense it.

(3) Import psilocybin or psilocin into the USA, or export either out of the USA.

Analogues

IN 1986, as part of the Anti-Drug Abuse Act of that year, "controlled substance analogues" were outlawed. They were vaguely defined as substances "intended for human consumption," and:

(1) the chemical structure of which is "substantially similar" to the chemical structure of a controlled substance in Schedule I or II;

(2) which have a stimulant, depressant, or hallucinogenic effect on the central nervous system that is "substantially similar" to or greater than the stimulant, depressant, or hallucinogenic effect on the central nervous system of a controlled substance in Schedule I or II; or

(3) with respect to a particular person, which such person represents or intends to have a stimulant, depressant, or hallucinogenic effect on the central nervous system that is "substantially similar" to or greater than the stimulant, depressant, or hallucinogenic effect on the central nervous system of a controlled substance in Schedule I or II.

Court Interpretation

AT LEAST ONE federal district court has held that to meet the tripartite definition of a "controlled substance analogue" [21 U.S.C. sec. 802, subd. (32)(A); 21 U.S.C. sec. 813.] a substance must meet the first prong *in combination with* either the second or third prong.

The substances baeocystine (4-phosphoryloxy-N-methyltryptamine) and norbaeocystine (4-phosphoryloxy-tryptamine), both *unscheduled* endogenous mushroom "toxins," have chemical structures similar to psilocybin and psilocin, and may also produce entheogenic effects. Consequently, under the analogue provisions of the CSA, both baeocystine and norbaeocystine would likely be considered illegal analogues of psilocybin and psilocin if possessed by someone intent on consuming them.

Likewise, in conjunction with an intent to consume them for their entheogenic properties, the unscheduled synthetic substances CY-19 (4-phosphoryloxy-*N*,*N*-diethyltryptamine), and CZ-74 (4-hydroxy-N,N-diethyltryptamine) would very likely also be considered analogues of psilocybin and psilocin.

Simple Possession

A PERSON CONVICTED of possessing psilocybin or psilocin *for his or her own use* is punished without regard to the amount—by weight—of the substances found in his or her possession. In practice, however, a person found with a moderate-to-large amount of any illegal drug will surely be charged with, and perhaps convicted of, the much more harshly punished crime of possession *with intent to distribute*. The crime of possession with intent to distribute is commonly called "possession for sale" or simply "sales." Note, however, that under federal law even giving away a scheduled substance is a crime, and hence using the word "sales" to denote the federal crime is a misnomer.

Quantity Presumed for Sale

HOW MUCH of a given substance is required to raise a presumption of intent to distribute varies from jurisdiction to jurisdiction and case to case. The presumption can be rebutted, but the burden to do so is on the defendant.

First Conviction

A PERSON who suffers a federal conviction for simple possession of psilocybin or psilocin is punished the same today as in 1968: a *mandatory* fine of $1,000 and anywhere from no incarceration up to imprisonment for a maximum of one year.

Second Conviction

ON A SECOND CONVICTION, a federal court must impose a *mandatory minimum* of fifteen days incarceration and a fine of at least $2,500. The maximum term that a federal court can impose for a second conviction is two years imprisonment.

Third Conviction

A THIRD CONVICTION triggers a *mandatory minimum* of 90 days imprisonment and a fine of at least $5,000. The maximum term that the federal court can impose for a third conviction is three years imprisonment.

These punishments can be increased or "enhanced"—often dramatically—for various reasons, including: "using" a weapon in commission of the offense—often simply having one in the same room; employing a minor in commission of the offense; committing the offense within 1,000 feet of a school, etc.

Manufacturing, Distributing, or Trafficking

A PERSON SUFFERING a federal conviction for manufacturing, distributing, trafficking, importing, or exporting psilocybin or psilocin—as distinct from simple possession for one's own use will have his or her sentence determined under the federal sentencing guidelines. The guidelines are extremely complex, requiring the consideration of a multitude of factors that can increase or decrease a person's sentence.

The guidelines were designed to increase the uniformity and fairness of sentencing in federal criminal cases. To implement this aim, sentences for drug crimes are largely determined by using marijuana sentences as a benchmark. The punishment for non-marijuana drug crimes is determined by utilizing a "drug equivalency table" which lists various outlawed substances and artificially equates them to marijuana. Under the drug equivalency table, 1 gram of psilocin or psilocybin is equated to 500 grams of marijuana.

For example, determining the federal punishment of someone convicted of distributing psilocybin is accomplished by taking the amount of psilocybin—by weight—and, using the equivalency table, converting it to its marijuana equivalent. The defendant is then punished as if he or she had been convicted of distributing the resultant amount of marijuana.

For use only in those offenses where no substance was recovered by the authorities (for example, if a person were arrested just after negotiating to sell "*x* doses" of psilocybin or psilocin, but *before* any actual substance was transferred), the guidelines decree a "typical weight per dose" of psilocybin or psilocin based on information supplied by the Drug Enforcement Administration. Both psilocybin and psilocin—in their pure chemical forms—are assigned the same "typical weight per dose" of 10 mg.

If the conviction involved *mushrooms* that contain the substances *and* the mushrooms are recovered by the authorities, the sentence is determined by equating one gram of dried mushrooms to one gram of marijuana. One gram of wet mushrooms are, however, equated to 0.1 gram of marijuana. The equivalent marijuana sentence is then determined from the guidelines.

The weight per dose table specifically lists *Psilocybe* mushrooms by genus name. Dry *Psilocybe* mushrooms are assigned a typical weight per dose of 5 grams, and wet *Psilocybe* mushrooms a typical weight per dose of 50 grams.

Calculating Punishment

TABLES 1 AND 2 that follow are derived from the federal sentencing guidelines. They simplify the procedure of sentence determination by having already made the necessary marijuana equation.

To determine the punishment for a *first-time* Federal offender, simply find the amount of the specific substance–chemicals, dry mushrooms, or wet mushrooms–in Table 1 and determine the associated offense level. Then, using Table 2, find the federal punishment range for that offense level.

For *simple possession* there is no need to use the tables. The federal punishment is uniform for simple possession, without regard to the quantity of the substance.

TABLE 1

Offense levels for federal crimes of manufacturing, distributing, trafficking, importing or exporting psilocybin or psilocin.

CONTROLLED SUBSTANCES PSILOCYBIN OR PSILOCIN

Amount by Weight	Offense Level
Less than 10 grams (gm)	Level 12
10 gm but less than 20 gm	Level 14
20 gm but less than 40 gm	Level 16
40 gm but less than 80 gm	Level 18
80 gm but less than 120 gm	Level 20
120 gm but less than 160 gm	Level 22
160 gm but less than 200 gm	Level 24
200 gm but less than 800 gm	Level 26
80 gm but less than 1.4 kilo (kg)	Level 28
1.4 kg but less than 2.0 kg	Level 30
2.0 kg but less than 6.0 kg	Level 32
6.0 kg but less than 20 kg	Level 34
20 kg but less than 60 kg	Level 36
60 kg but less than 200 kg	Level 38
200 kg but less than 600 kg	Level 40
600 kg or more	Level 42

DRY MUSHROOMS CONTAINING PSILOCYBIN OR PSILOCIN

Amount by Weight	Offense Level
2.5 kg but less than 5 kg	Level 12
5 kg but less than 10 kg	Level 14
10 kg but less than 20 kg	Level 16
20 kg but less than 40 kg	Level 18
40 kg but less than 60 kg	Level 20
60 kg but less than 80 kg	Level 22
80 kg but less than 100 kg	Level 24
100 kg but less than 400 kg	Level 26
400 kg but less than 700 kg	Level 28
700 kg but less than 1,000 kg	Level 30
1,000 kg but less than 3,000 kg	Level 32
3,000 kg but less than 10,000 kg	Level 34
10,000 kg but less than 30,000 kg	Level 36
30,000 kg but less than 100,000 kg	Level 38
100,000 kg but less than 300,000 kg	Level 40
300,000 kg or more	Level 42

Wet mushrooms containing psilocybin or psilocin

Amount by Weight	Offense Level
Less than 50 kg	Level 12
50 kg but less than 100 kg	Level 14
100 kg but less than 200 kg	Level 16
200 kg but less than 400 kg	Level 18
400 kg but less than 600 kg	Level 20
600 kg but less than 800 kg	Level 22
800 kg but less than 1,000 kg	Level 24
1,000 kg but less than 4,000 kg	Level 26
4,000 kg but less than 7,000 kg	Level 28
7,000 kg but less than 10,000 kg	level 30
10,000 kg but less than 30,000 kg	Level 32
30,000 kg but less than 100,000 kg	Level 34
100,000 kg but less than 300,000 kg	Level 36
300,000 kg but less than 1,000,000 kg	Level 38
1,000,000 kg but less than 3,000,000 kg	Level 40
3,000,000 kg or more	Level 42

Table 2

Federal punishment by offense level

Offense Level	Prison Term in Months	Fine in $1,000s
Level 12	10 to 16	$3 to $30
Level 14	15 to 21	$4 to $40
Level 16	21 to 27	$5 to $50
Level 18	27 to 33	$6 to $60
Level 20	33 to 41	$7.5 to $75
Level 22	41 to 51	$7.5 to $75
Level 24	51 to 63	$10 to $100
Level 26	63 to 78	$12.5 to $125
Level 28	78 to 97	$12.5 to $125
Level 30	97 to 121	$15 to $150
Level 32	121 to 151	$17.5 to $175
Level 34	151 to 188	$17.5 to $175
Level 36	188 to 235	$20 to $200
level 38	235 to 293	$25 to $250
Level 40	192 to 365	$25 to $250
Level 42	360 to life	$25 to $250

4

State Law

IN ADDITION TO BEING CONTROLLED under federal law, psilocybin and psilocin are currently controlled substances in every state. State crimes involving the substances were delineated in the Model Controlled Substances Act of 1970, an act modeled on the federal Controlled Substance Act.

Although the Model Act was designed to provide uniformity among the various states' drug crimes and punishments, many states that have adopted the Model Act have gone on to make extensive modifications. Nevertheless, while the specifics of the various drug crimes and their associated punishment may vary from state to state, *every* state makes it a crime to: possess psilocybin or psilocin, or to distribute, sell, or manufacture these substances.

Calculating State Punishment

TABLE 3 INDICATES the maximum state punishments for a first conviction involving psilocybin or psilocin. The column headed "DL Lost" indicates that *any* drug conviction–even if no vehicle was involved in the offense–results in suspension of one's driving privilege, usually for six months.

TABLE 3

Maximum State Punishment for First Conviction Involving Psilocybin or Psilocin.

State	DL Lost	Possession in $1000s	Sale/Cultivation
Alabama	Y	Life/$500K	Life/$500K
Alaska	N	5yrs/$50K	20yrs/$50K
Arizona	N	4yrs/$1K-$150K	7yrs/$1K-$150K
Arkansas	Y	3-10yrs/$10K	life/$100K
California	N	3yrs/ $20K	9yrs/$20K
Colorado	Y	12yrs/$3K-$750K	12yrs/$3K-$750K
Connecticut	Y	7 yrs/$50K	15yrs/$50K
Delaware	Y	15yrs/$400K	15yrs/$1K-$400K
DC	Y	180 days/$1K	5yrs/$50K
Florida	Y	30yrs/$10K	74yrs/$500K
Georgia	Y	25 yrs/$1000K	30yrs/$500 K
Hawaii	N	20 yrs/$50K	20yrs/$50K
Idaho	N	3 yrs/$5K	5 yrs/$15K
Illinois	Y	50 yrs/$200K	60 yrs/$500K
Indiana	Y	1.5yrs/$10K	10yrs/$10K
Iowa	N	1yrs/$250-$1.5K	10yrs/$1K-$50K
Kansas	Y	1yrs/$2.5K	16 mo/$300
Kentucky	N	1 yrs/$500	5 yrs/$1K-$10K
Louisiana	Y	20yrs/$5K	30 yrs/$50K
Maine	N	1yrs/$2K	5yrs/$5K
Massachusetts	Y	1yrs/$1K	5yrs/$500-$5K
Maryland	N	4yrs/$25K	25yrs/$50K
Michigan	Y	2yrs/$2K	7yrs/$10K
Minnesota	Y	30yrs/$1000K	35 yrs/$1250K
Mississippi	Y	3yrs/$1K-$30K	life/$5K-$1000K

(Maximum State Punishment continued)

State	DL Lost	Possession in $1000s	Sale/Cultivation
Missouri	N	life/$5K	life/$5K
Montana	Y	5 yrs/$50K	Life/$50K
Nebraska	N	5 yrs/$10K	50yrs/$25K
Nevada	N	life/$500K	life/$500K
N Hampshire	Y	7yrs/$25K	7yrs/$100K
New Jersey	Y	5yrs/$35 K	20yrs/$500K
New Mexico	N	1yrs/$500-$1K	3yrs/$5K
New York	Y	Life/$50K	Life/$50K
N Carolina	N	23yrs	23yrs
N Dakota	N	5yrs/$5K	20yrs/$10K
Ohio	Y	10yrs/$20K	10yrs/$20K
Oklahoma	Y	15yrs/$250K	6 mo-$250K
Oregon	N	10yrs/$200K	20 yrs/$300K
Pennsylvania	Y	1yrs/$5K	10yrs/$100K
Rhode Is	Y	3yrs/$500-$5K	Life/$3K-$1000K
S Carolina	Y	25yrs/$100K	25yrs/$100K
S Dakota	Y	5yrs/$5K	1-10 yrs/$10K
Tennessee	N	1yrs/$2.5K	8-60yrs/$2K$500K
Texas	Y	6mo–life/$100K	6mo-life/$250K
Utah	Y	5yrs/$5K	1-15yrs/$10K
Vermont	N	15yrs/$500K	15yrs/$500K
Virginia	Y	10yrs/$2.5K	5-40yrs/$500K
Washington	N	5yrs/$10K	5yrs/$10K
W Virginia	N	90dy-6mo/$1K	1-5yrs/$15K
Wisconsin	Y	1yrs/$5K	30yrs/$1000K
Wyoming	N	5yrs/$10K	10yrs/$10K

Unless a defendant makes it an issue, most state courts do *not* distinguish *the substances* psilocybin and psilocin from *mushrooms* that naturally embody these substances. Therefore, Table 2 can be used to determine the potential maximum state punishment for possession, sale or cultivation of *mushrooms* that endogenously produce psilocybin or psilocin.

5

Spores & Growing Kits

THE ENDOGENOUS ALKALOIDS psilocybin and psilocin are produced as the mushroom matures, first becoming detectable in most cases during the mycelial stage of development. Neither substance exists in the spores of the mushrooms, giving rise to numerous commercial enterprises that sell spores and "mushroom growing kits." Because the spores are not expressly outlawed under federal law—nor can they possibly be considered a "mixture" containing a controlled substance because they contain no psilocybin or psilocin—they are legal everywhere except California and Georgia. Only those two states have passed laws that target mushroom spores.

Anti-Spore Laws

GEORGIA'S LIST of "dangerous drugs" explicitly includes "mushroom spores which, when mature, contain either psilocybin or psilocin." With limited exceptions for licensed pharmacies, doctors, and pharmaceutical companies, it is a misdemeanor "for any person, firm, corporation, or association to sell, give away, barter, exchange, distribute, or possess" such mushroom spores in Georgia. The offense is punishable by a maximum fine of $1,000 and/or up to twelve months in county jail. [Georgia Code: 16-13-71(b)(627); 16-13-56; 17-10-3]

California's anti-spore laws were enacted in 1985, defining a multitude of crimes related to mushroom spores and mycelia "capable of producing mushrooms containing the controlled substances" psilocybin and the misnamed "psilocyn." The California statutes read as follows:

> SECTION 11390: cultivation of spores or mycelium capable of producing mushrooms or other material containing controlled substance; punishment
>
> Except as otherwise authorized by law, every person who, with intent to produce a controlled substance specified in paragraph (18) [psilocybin] or (19) [psilocyn] [*sic*] of subdivision (d) of Section 11054, cultivates any spores or mycelium capable of producing mushrooms or other material which contains such a controlled substance shall be punished by imprisonment in the county jail for a period of not more than one year or in the state prison.

SECTION 11391: transporting, importing, selling, furnishing, giving away, etc., spores or mycelium capable of producing mushrooms containing controlled substance to violate sec. 11390; punishment

Except as otherwise authorized by law, every person who transports, imports into this state, sells, furnishes, gives away, or offers to transport, import into this state, sell, furnish, or give away any spores or mycelium capable of producing mushrooms or other material which contain a controlled substance specified in paragraph (18) [psilocybin] or (19) [psilocyn] [*sic*] of subdivision (d) of Section 11054 for the purpose of facilitating a violation of Section 11390 shall be punished by imprisonment in the county jail for a period of not more than one year or in the state prison.

SECTION 11392: spores or mycelium capable of producing mushrooms or other material containing psilocyn [*sic*] or psyocylin [*sic*]; use in research, instruction, or analysis

Spores or mycelium capable of producing mushrooms or other material which contains psilocyn [*sic*] or psyocylin [*sic*] may be lawfully obtained and used for bona fide research, instruction, or analysis, if not in violation of federal law, and if the research, instruction, or analysis is approved by the Research Advisory Panel established pursuant to Sections 11480 and 11481.

Under the above statutes a prosecutor could charge a person with a felony for importing psilocybian mushroom spores into California. A first conviction under section 11390 or section 11391 is punishable by a maximum of one year in county jail or state prison.

A Small Loophole

UNDER THE PLAIN TERMS of the statutes, actions involving spores are only a crime if done "for the purpose of producing mushrooms or other materials which contain a controlled substance." In other words, it appears that it is perfectly legal to import *Psilocybe* mushrooms spores into California or sell them, so long as the spores are not intended to be used for cultivation. So, importing *Psilocybe* spore prints for the purpose of assisting mushroom identification, or for viewing the spore's natural beauty,– or for any reason other than to facilitate cultivation–appears to be technically legal, even in California.

It is dangerous to do so, however, because the average drug enforcement agent or prosecutor, upon learning that someone in California was importing *Psilocybe* spore prints, would probably jump to the conclusion that the person intends to cultivate the mushroom for its "hallucinatory" properties. A defendant facing such a charge would likely have a very hard time convincing a jury that his or her importation of *Psilocybe* spores–especially from a company advertising in *High Times*–was not accompanied by the intent to cultivate the mushrooms for their visionary powers.

Mail-Order Investigations

IN THE LATE 1980S the DEA subpoenaed the customer records of various mail order companies selling hydroponic equipment and indoor grow lights. The information led to dozens of marijuana-related arrests. In 1993, a man named Tab Deaner was convicted, based, in part, on his mail-orders.

The following information was revealed in the court's opinion:

> "Deaner became a suspect after the DEA learned that he had made mail order purchases...from Wormsway Organic Indoor/Outdoor Garden Supply (Wormsway). [DEA agent] Andrasi related in the affidavit that he learned...that Wormsway was a supplier of cultivation equipment seized in various indoor marijuana cultivation operations, and that Wormsway was an advertiser in *High Times* magazine. Andrasi also stated that undercover agents had discussed marijuana cultivation with Wormsway's owner...."

Andrasi reviewed UPS shipping records which indicated that Deaner had received five packages from Wormsway at regular intervals over an eight month period. Andrasi said this regular flow of packages from Wormsway supported his belief that Deaner was cultivating marijuana." (US v. Deaner (3rd Cir. 1993) 1 F.3d 192.)

Spore Risks

EVEN IN STATES where mushroom spores are ostensibly legal to possess and sell, there is a legal risk to selling or buying them. In early May 1994, Alaska drug enforcement agents, armed with a search warrant, raided Power Products, an Alaska company selling *Psilocybe cubensis* mushroom growing kits. During the search, agents seized: books, glass jars, letters, and business records, including a log-book of all people–estimated at approximately 600–who corresponded with the company or ordered mushroom growing kits since the company began doing business in March 1993.

The raid was evidently the result of a Washington man who alerted authorities after finding his fourteen-year-old daughter in possession of either a Power Products' growing kit, or mushrooms produced by such a kit. Washington drug enforcement agents then traced the kit to Power Products in Juneau, Alaska.

In an unfortunate twist, approximately three months before the raid, the proprietor of Power Products was arrested for receiving marijuana in the mail, which he was importing to aid a friend suffering from AIDS. The marijuana case was set for trial when the Power Products raid occurred.

The prosecutor handling the marijuana case threatened to introduce evidence related to the Power Products raid in an effort to paint the proprietor as a major "drug dealer," thereby negating his defense that the marijuana was solely intended for the man's ailing friend. The prosecutor also threatened to charge the proprietor with multiple felony counts arising from the Power Products raid, including: psilocybin distribution, aiding and abetting misconduct related to a controlled substance, and contributing to the delinquency of a minor.

Feeling the pressure of these threats, the proprietor of Power Products agreed to settle both cases by pleading guilty to a single count of misconduct involving a controlled substance in the fourth degree, a crime carrying a maximum sentence of five years in state prison and a maximum fine of $50,000.

Customer Lists

Power Products advertised in *High Times* magazine as well as *Psychedelic Illuminations.* The raid garnered the Alaska authorities a list of names and addresses for as many as 600 people who wrote to, or ordered products from Power Products. Although these people broke no laws by ordering from, or corresponding with, the company, their names and addresses fell into the hands of law enforcement agents.

There have been instances in the past where authorities have obtained the order lists of companies selling hydroponic growing equipment through advertisements in *High Times.* In several such cases, the authorities used the information to trigger investigations of the people who placed orders. Often the first step in such an investigation is to run all the names through a network law enforcement computer system to see if any of the people have a prior conviction for a drug offense. If a "hit" is made, the authorities will sometimes show up unannounced to search the person and his or her home under the authority of a search and seizure waiver that is commonly a condition of probation or parole on a drug case.

In almost all circumstances, however, simply placing an order from a company selling mushroom spores will not–by itself–give the authorities enough to obtain a search warrant for the home of the person who made the order. Additional factors reasonably indicating that the person is *currently* engaging in criminal conduct are necessary before an officer could obtain a valid search warrant.

Intercepted Letters

REGARDING SEIZED LETTERS that might detail mycological activities of the writer, the authorities will often use such documents as the first tip to begin investigating the letter writer. The depth of the investigation depends on the content of the letter. Recently-dated letters mentioning an ongoing growing operation will prompt the most attention. Therefore, people who write letters to, or purchase supplies from a mushroom spore company should be able to rest easy even in the event the company is raided, so long as several months have passed from the time of correspondence or purchase. Those most at risk in the event a company is raided would be those people who placed orders or received shipments in the several weeks immediately before the raid.

PART II

Court Decisions

6

The Allen Case

GLEN ALLEN WAS ARRESTED by federal agents after United States Postal Inspectors, employing a "drug package profile" discovered LSD in an "express mail package" sent cross-country. The arrest of the person who claimed the package subsequently led agents to find psilocybian mushrooms in a barn on Mr. Allen's family property.

Mr. Allen was prosecuted for possession of psilocybin; the primary evidence being the mushrooms seized from the barn. The agents also presented testimony of a person who claimed that he asked Mr. Allen whether he could get him some "psilocybin," and that Mr. Allen offered him the mushrooms in his barn for $250 per quarter pound. Based on this evidence, Mr. Allen was convicted of the federal crime of possessing psilocybin with the intent to distribute. The conviction was upheld by the First Circuit Court of Appeals. [*U.S. v. Allen* (1st Cir. 1993) 990 F.2d 667].

Drug Package Profile

THE "DRUG PACKAGE PROFILE" is a compilation of characteristics which mail handlers (public and private) have come to associate with packages that contain illegal drugs. Such packages receive heightened scrutiny by postal authorities and run a greater chance of being presented to a drug-sniffing dog.

PROFILE OF A SUSPECTED DRUG PACKAGE

The package is sent express, overnight, or priority via a public or private carrier;
The package is sent from or to a known "source state" for drugs;
The package is sent from one individual to another individual;
The mailing labels are hand-written;
The return address is fictitious or inaccurate;
There are unusual odors coming from the package;
The package is heavily taped to seal all openings.

One tragic aspect of Mr. Allen's case is that it appears that no one ever made the argument that the *mushrooms* themselves were not scheduled substances under federal law and could not be equated to the outlawed substance psilocybin.

The handling of this case underscores the crucial need to seek expert legal representation if ever charged with a mushroom or other entheogen-related crime. The good news about the *Allen* case is that because the substance-versus-mushroom argument was not raised or decided, it remains viable, and could serve as a defense in a future federal prosecution for possession of mushrooms that naturally contain psilocybin.

7

The Fiske Case

THE FIRST PUBLISHED *state* case directly addressing the issue of *mushroom* legality was issued by the Florida Supreme Court in 1978. The case involved Richard Fiske, who was arrested as he emerged from a field in Collier County, Florida. It is not clear from the opinion, but it appears that he was initially arrested for trespassing. Near him, the officers found a bag of freshly picked wild mushrooms, which laboratory testing showed to naturally contain psilocybin. Following a jury trial, Mr. Fiske was found guilty of possessing psilocybin in violation of Florida law. [*Fiske v. State* (Fla. 1978) 366 So.2d 423].

Richard Fiske's conviction was reversed by the Florida Supreme Court after he successfully argued that the Florida statute, which only explicitly outlawed *the substance* psilocybin and said nothing about mushrooms, violated his federal and state constitutional rights to due process when said to criminalize his possession of unscheduled wild mushrooms.

Florida Supreme Court

THE FLORIDA SUPREME COURT reached its decision by examining the language of the Florida statute that placed in Schedule I, "any material which contains a quantity of the hallucinogenic substance psilocybin." Holding that it was unconstitutional to apply the statute to wild mushrooms, the court explained:

> The statute makes no mention of psilocybic mushrooms or, for that matter, of any other psilocybic organic form that grows wild. If the statute were to specify that psilocybin was contained in certain identifiable mushrooms and were to name those mushrooms as unlawful, it would not be unconstitutional as applied. The statute as presently framed, however, gives no information as to what plants may contain psilocybin in its natural state. More particularly, the statute does not advise a person of ordinary and common intelligence that this substance is contained in a particular variety of mushroom. The statute, therefore, may not be applied constitutionally to [Mr. Fiske]. It does not give fair warning that the mushrooms possessed by appellant is a crime.
>
> There is no vagueness problem with the statute on its face. It explicitly controls any material which contains psilocybin and makes possession of the material a felony. In capsule, pill, or similar form, the statute may be applied constitutionally for people will be wary of the criminal liabilities of possession of nonprescribed drugs in their common medicinal forms and will not ordinarily possess them innocently or without knowing of their content.

In short, the Florida Supreme Court recognized that *Psilocybe* mushrooms are distinct from pills or capsules containing psilocybin and psilocin. For the purposes of the state's anti-drug law, only the latter were properly considered "materials which contain psilocyin [*sic*]."

To this day, *Fiske* remains the strongest case supporting a legal distinction between the expressly scheduled *substances* psilocybin and psilocin, and the unscheduled *mushrooms* that naturally embody those chemicals.

8

The Dunlap Case

THE REASONING in the *Fiske* case was examined, but rejected, in an Illinois case decided in 1982. There, two men were charged with numerous state drug crimes after agents seized *Psilocybe* mushrooms from the home of one of the men. [*People v. Dunlap* (Ill. App. 1982) 442 N.E.2d 1379].

The men moved to dismiss the charges on the ground that their activities with *Psilocybe* mushrooms did not violate any criminal law. The trial court agreed with the men, finding that while Illinois law, like that in Florida, outlawed psilocybin and psilocin, it did not specifically outlaw any mushrooms. The trial court also held that the cultivation of *Psilocybe* mushrooms was not illegal under the Illinois definition of *manufacture*. As a result, the trial court dismissed the charges against the men. But, the state appealed.

The Illinois appellate court reversed the trial court, accepting the government's "mushrooms-are-materials" argument. The appellate court explained that Illinois included within Schedule I, "any material . . . which contains any quantity of . . . psilocyn [*sic*]." These words, held the appellate court, "mean exactly that–any such material is a Schedule I substance, and thus mushrooms which, in their natural state, contain psilocin [*sic*], are included in Schedule I."

Manufacturing

THE ILLINOIS APPELLATE COURT then examined the state's statutory definition of *manufacture*, which prohibited "the production, preparation, propagation, compounding, conversion or processing of a controlled substance, either directly of indirectly, by extraction from substances of natural origin, or independently by means of chemical synthesis . . . ."

While the state's definition of *manufacture* made no mention of cultivation, the court pointed to the statutory definition of *production* which proscribed the "planting, cultivating, growing, or harvesting of a controlled substance." Accordingly, the court concluded that simply growing a *Psilocybe* mushroom was equivalent to illegally producing a controlled substance:

> It has been stated that, by itself, the definition of *manufacture* might suggest that that term refers only to extraction, chemical synthesis or a combination thereof, but when read with the definition of *production*, it is apparent that the *growing* of plant matter containing a controlled substance is prohibited.

The appellate court also rejected the argument that the statute violated due process by failing to give adequate notice that possession of certain mushroom species was a crime. The court found no due process violation and rejected the contrary reasoning by the Florida Supreme Court in Richard Fiske's case:

> ...the *Fiske* majority...held, by implication, that the only natural reading of the phrase "any material" would be limited to a controlled substance "in capsule, pill or similar form." ...In our view, this is an overly restrictive and artificial interpretation of that language. In fact, the term "material" is more commonly used to refer to an item which is the source of something else rather than a finished product (See *Webster's Third New International Dictionary*, "material"), and thus,..a person of ordinary intelligence would be amply apprised by [the Illinois law] that possession of *Psilocybe* mushrooms is illegal. As applied to one possessing mushrooms known to contain psilocyn [*sic*], the [Illinois] Controlled Substances Act is not unconstitutional.

Knowledge Required

THE ILLINOIS APPELLATE COURT noted, however, that truly naive mushroom cultivators or hunters were protected from conviction because a conviction required proof that the person possessing or cultivating the mushrooms *knew* they contained a controlled substance:

> An individual who cultivates or otherwise possessed *Psilocybe* mushrooms without knowing them to contain psilocyn *[sic]* would not be prosecuted successfully...because in a prosecution for the

possession or sale of controlled substances, the State must prove that a defendant had knowledge of the nature of the substance possessed or sold.

Schedule I Appropriate

LASTLY, the appellate court rejected the argument that the classification of psilocin as a Schedule I substance was irrational. Acknowledging that research on the effects of psilocin "is not plentiful," the court held "[n]onetheless, it is not the case that some facts do not exist to support the General Assembly's decision to place psilocyn [*sic*] along with the other major hallucinogens in Schedule I."

As a result of the above findings, the Illinois court of appeal concluded that the state's Controlled Substances Act "prohibits the knowing possession of mushrooms containing psilocyn [*sic*] ...and is not unconstitutional for so doing." Consequently, the court of appeal reversed the trial court and reinstated the charges against the men.

THE NO-KNOWLEDGE DEFENSE

In most states, possession of Psilocybe *mushrooms without knowledge that they contain controlled substances is not a crime. Readers are cautioned, however, that most jurors will quickly find that a defendant caught possessing or cultivating* Psilocybe *mushrooms knew that they endogenously produced a controlled substance.*

9

Patterson Case

TWO YEARS AFTER THE ILLINOIS DECISION in the Dunlap Case, an appellate court in the State of Washington was presented with a similar issue on appeal. Agents executing a search warrant at Douglas Patterson's home in Bellingham, Washington, found "4,400 Mason jars containing psilocybin mushrooms." Following a trial, Mr. Patterson was convicted of unlawful possession of a controlled substance and unlawful possession of a controlled substance with intent to deliver.

Mr. Patterson's appeal raised several issues, including the argument that "possession of any material containing psilocybin, does not include a natural plant which contains that chemical." He contended that because the Washington statute did not explicitly list mushrooms as controlled substances, the state's legislators never intended to criminalize the possession of mushrooms.

Interestingly, agents first learned that Mr. Patterson was cultivating mushrooms after arresting a burglar who broke into Mr. Patterson's home. In exchange for more lenient treatment, the burglar told the agents that while burglarizing Mr. Patterson's home he found what he believed was an illegal mushroom growing operation and took some of the mushrooms. The burglar gave some of these mushrooms–which were indeed found to contain psilocybin–to the agents, and they subsequently used them to obtain a search warrant for Mr. Patterson's home. [*State v. Patterson* (Wash. App. 1984, 679 P.2d 416)].

The Washington appellate court accepted the prosecutor's "mushrooms-are-materials" argument:

> The words of the statute have an unambiguous meaning that does not permit subjective interpretation. The [statute] makes it unlawful to 'possess...a controlled substance." "Controlled substance" is defined to include a "substance . . . in Schedules I through V..." Schedule I includes "any material . . . which contains any quantity of...[p]silocybin." The key word "material" means "consisting of matter." *Webster's Third New Int'l Dictionary* [pg. 1392, 1976]. This meaning is sufficiently explicit to include substances in their natural state as well as chemical derivatives or compounds. We conclude that it was the clear legislative intent to include the psilocybin mushroom as a controlled substance.

Strict Liablity

THE WASHINGTON COURT distinguished the Florida Supreme Court's decision in Richard Fiske's case by explaining that, unlike the Florida law, guilt under the Washington law did *not* require proof of the defendant's knowledge or intent.

The State of Washington is unique in fashioning anti-drug laws that essentially impose strict liability for unauthorized possession of controlled substances. *State v. Cleppe* (Wash. 1981, 635 P.2d 435) held that the statute forbidding possession of a controlled substance does not require proof of guilty knowledge. The *Cleppe* court, however, left open the use of an affirmative defense of "unwitting possession." [*See State v. Hundley* (Wash. App. 1994, 866 P.2d 56)] reversal of drug conviction based on affirmative defense of "unwitting possession".

10

The Justice Case

THE QUESTION of psilocybian mushrooms' legality came before a Kansas court of appeal in 1985. There, Jon Justice unwittingly negotiated to sell mushrooms to an undercover Sheriff's deputy. Although Mr. Justice never mentioned that the mushrooms specifically contained psilocybin, he did state on several occasions that the mushrooms were "strong," "got you high," and "made you closer to God." He was arrested after he sold some of the mushrooms–which were later confirmed to contain psilocybin–to the deputy. [*State v. Justice* (Kans. 1985) 704 P.2d 1012]

Mr. Justice was convicted and appealed, arguing that the Kansas law outlawing the possession of the substance psilocybin was unconstitutionally vague when applied to someone who possessed mushrooms, rather than the pure chemical. In particular, he pointed out that the Kansas Legislature had been very clear in explicitly outlawing *the plant sources* of marijuana, opium, and mescaline, in addition to their active principles. Had the Kansas Legislature intended to outlaw *Psilocybe* mushrooms, he argued, it would have expressly done so, rather than simply outlawing the chemicals psilocybin and psilocin:

> Defendant contends that by contrast to the other hallucinogens listed in [the Kansas statute] psilocybin and psilocyn [*sic*] are the only ones with a major natural source, *Psilocybe* mushrooms, which are not clearly identified in the statute. He argues that this deficiency, in light of the specificity with which other controlled substances are described, creates doubt whether the mushrooms naturally containing psilocybin were intended to be controlled. This doubt, he contends, evidences the statute's failure to provide adequate notice that possession for sale of a mushroom containing psilocybin is prohibited.

The Kansas court of appeal answered Mr. Justice's argument by adopting the reasoning of the courts in the Illinois and Washington decisions discussed earlier. The Kansas court explained:

> ...use of the phrase "any material...which contains" psilocybin, provides ample notice that *mushrooms* containing psilocybin are controlled. Moreover, in light of the use of the catch-all language "any material," it cannot be said that uncertainty is created by the listing of other controlled substances by both the name of the substance and its natural source. Perhaps the legislature could have drafted a statute listing the score of mushroom species known to contain psilocybin, but failure to use more precise language to accomplish an identical goal does not render the existing law unconstitutionally vague.

11

The Wohlever Case

AN OHIO COURT OF APPEALS issued an opinion in 1985 on the subject of substances versus mushrooms. In that case, Johna Wohlever was charged with aggravated trafficking in drugs, in violation of Ohio law. The indictment against her read:

> "the defendant knowingly sold or offered to sell a controlled substance, to wit: *Psilocybe* Mushrooms, a Schedule I controlled substance.... "

A jury found her guilty and she appealed, arguing that the indictment failed to state a crime:

> "Defendant argues that *Psilocybe* mushrooms are not one of the controlled substances listed in Schedule I of [the Ohio Controlled Substances Act]; hence, an essential element in the crime of drug trafficking is missing from the indictment." [*State v. Wohlever* (Ohio App. 1985) 500 N.E.2d 318.]

The Ohio court of appeals agreed with Ms. Wohlever's argument and reversed her conviction. The holding, however, was based on a unique rule earlier set down by the Ohio Supreme Court requiring indictments in that state to specifically name the controlled substance involved. The court of appeal, noting that Ms. Wohlever's indictment alleged that she sold or offered to sell "*Psilocybe* Mushrooms, a Schedule I controlled substance," explained:

> But *Psilocybe* mushrooms are not among the substances listed in R.C. 3719.41 and possession of *Psilocybe* mushrooms is nowhere proscribed. Further, the state does not dispute that there are species of *Psilocybe* mushrooms which contain no hallucinogens. Psilocybin and psilocyn [*sic*] are controlled substances listed under Schedule I.... But the indictment here not only does not mention these specific substances, it does not name the type of substance–hallucinogens . . . . The legislature has clearly detailed substances which are controlled and *Psilocybe* mushrooms are not among them.

12

The Kail Case

A COURT OF APPEAL IN INDIANA upheld the conviction of Kenneth Kail for possession of psilocin in 1988. In the court of appeal, Mr. Kail admitted that he possessed some *mushrooms*, but he argued that the prosecutor failed to prove that he knowingly possessed *psilocin*. [*Kail v. State* (Ind. App.1 Dist. 1988) 528 N.E.2d 799.]

The court of appeal agreed that in order to convict Mr. Kail of possessing psilocin naturally occurring in mushrooms, the state was required to prove that Mr. Kail knew that the mushrooms in his possession contained the outlawed substance. That said, however, the court held that the prosecutor had met his burden of proof on that issue by presenting sufficient evidence for the jury to logically infer that Mr. Kail knew his mushrooms contained psilocin.

As proof of Mr. Kail's "criminal knowledge," the court of appeal pointed to the fact that the mushrooms were found in an overnight case that also contained over eight thousand dollars in cash. In the same bedroom that contained the mushrooms and cash, the police also found a large amount of marijuana, further indicating that Mr. Kail was not completely naive about illicit drugs.

The court also noted that a police chemist testified at Mr. Kail's trial that the mushrooms did not grow naturally in Indiana, but could be grown "artificially," or purchased on the street. Finally, the appellate court pointed out that using the mushrooms for the psychoactive properties required nothing more than ingesting them. "[F]rom this evidence," concluded the court of appeal, "the jury could reasonably infer that Kail knew the character of the mushrooms at the time he possessed them." This was sufficient for conviction.

13

The Bemis Case

THE ISSUE OF PSILOCYBIN ILLEGALITY versus psilocybian *mushroom* legality was addressed again by an Indiana court of appeals in 1995. Following a jury trial in 1993, Guy Bemis was convicted of "dealing psilocybin" and "possession of psilocybin," based on mushrooms found in his home. He was sentenced to six years imprisonment on the dealing conviction and a concurrent eighteen-month term on the possession conviction. Mr. Bemis appealed.

The Indiana court of appeals affirmed Mr. Bemis' convictions, holding that *Psilocybe* mushrooms were properly considered illegal "materials" containing the controlled substances psilocybin and psilocin. [*Bemis v. State* (Ind. App. 1995) 652 N.E.2d 89.]

The Indiana court of appeals summarized the facts leading to Mr. Bemis' arrest:

On September 4, 1992, Bemis met Sharon Mosby at a local bar in Evansville. Mosby left the bar with Bemis to go to his apartment. After arriving at the apartment, Bemis gave Mosby a bowl containing dried mushrooms. Mosby ate one mushroom and part of a second one. Despite Bemis' warning not to drive, Mosby left in her car. During Mosby's drive home, she began hallucinating and vomiting. When Mosby arrived home she was laughing and crying uncontrollably. Her son transported her to the Emergency room of St. Mary's Medical Center, where she explained the events of the evening to Evansville police officers.

Bemis consented to a search of his apartment on September 5, 1992. Police officers seized a Tupperware container which contained dried mushrooms. Police also seized other mushrooms that were growing throughout Bemis' apartment, massive amounts of paraphernalia associated with his mushroom growing operation, and various literature concerning mushroom growing and in-home drug cultivation. The mushrooms in the Tupperware container were later tested and found to contain [p]silocin.

The record further reveals that in August of 1992, Bemis telephoned Purdue University's county extension educator, Larry Kaplan, and asked him how to grow mushrooms and whether psilocybin mushrooms were edible. Kaplan testified at trial that during this conversation he informed Bemis that psilocybin mushrooms were hallucinogenic and illegal.

Prior to trial, Bemis moved to dismiss the [charges], arguing that the statutes under which he was charged were unconstitutionally vague. The trial court denied the motion, and the case proceeded to trial [where Bemis was convicted].

Vague Law

IN THE INDIANA COURT OF APPEALS, Mr. Bemis argued that the state statutes outlawing the substances psilocybin and psilocin made no mention of *mushrooms* and hence failed to adequately inform him–or anyone else–that certain species of mushroom were actually outlawed. Such vagueness in a criminal law, argued Bemis, violates the due process guarantees of the federal Constitution and the Indiana Constitution.

The Indiana court of appeals rejected Bemis' arguments and affirmed his conviction. The court held:

> The Indiana Controlled Substance Act as it relates to [p]silocybin and [p]silocyn [*sic*] is not unconstitutionally vague. Indiana's statutory scheme gives persons of ordinary intelligence fair warning of the prohibited conduct and does not encourage arbitrary or discriminatory enforcement. Thus, the statutes are not unconstitutionally vague, either on their face or as applied to Bemis.

Mushroom is a "Material"

IN REACHING ITS DECISION that the statute was not unconstitutionally vague, the court of appeals relied on language in the *Dunlap* case from Illinois, which held that a similar statutory provision gave people fair notice that mushrooms containing psilocybin were themselves illegal to possess. Without any further analysis, the Indiana court of appeals adopted the Illinois court's construction of the word "material," concluding that the Indiana statute was not unconstitutionally vague—and that mushrooms containing psilocybin were themselves outlawed hallucinogenic "materials."

Having Knowledge

HAVING HELD that a mushroom was a "material" within the statutory definition of a hallucinogenic substance, the Illinois court of appeal then examined whether there was sufficient evidence to prove that Mr. Bemis knew his mushrooms contained psilocybin. The court of appeal wasted no time finding that the evidence was sufficient to support the conclusion that Mr. Bemis knew the mushrooms contained psilocybin.

Along with the other evidence found in his apartment on the evening he was arrested, the police found some "incriminating literature" including *Psychedelic Chemistry, Sex and Drugs, Clandestine Drug Laboratories, High Times, The Anarchist Cookbook* and *The Mushroom Cultivator.* In addition the officers also found a document entitled *Psylocybe Fanaticus Culture and Mushroom Kit*, which explained how to grow *Psilocybe* mushrooms.

The facts surrounding Mr. Bemis' arrest, noted the court, were in stark contrast to the facts in the Florida case involving Richard Fiske:

> ...in [the *Fiske* case], there was a complete absence of evidence that the defendant knew that he

> possessed illegal mushrooms. The defendant was arrested as he emerged from a field carrying a bag of wild mushrooms. This situation is more susceptible to an innocent explanation than the factual situation in the case before us. In the case at bar, police seized from Bemis' apartment several items of paraphernalia used in cultivating mushrooms, publications on the subject of cultivating mushrooms, including psilocybic mushrooms, as well as several mushrooms growing throughout the apartment. Larry Kaplan also testified that he informed Bemis that psilocybic mushrooms were illegal and hallucinogenic.

Mr. Bemis' case is a good example of one in which the specific facts eclipsed the valid legal arguments. Given the incriminating items seized from his apartment, Mr. Bemis' strongest argument was not that *he* didn't know that the mushrooms contained psilocybin, but rather *on its face* the Indiana anti-drug statute was unconstitutionally vague if stretched to apply to life forms that endogenously produce controlled substances. This latter issue, being one of statutory interpretation, was largely independent of the difficult facts in Mr. Bemis' case.

14

The Ryan Case

ROBERT RYAN WAS CHARGED in New York in 1992 with attempted possession of a controlled substance after Federal Express employees found over 30 ounces of dried *Psilocybe* mushrooms inside a package mailed to him. [*People v. Ryan* (1992) 591 N.Y.S.2d 218.]

In his defense, Mr. Ryan argued that New York's law explicitly defined the offense of second degree possession as "knowingly and unlawfully possessing...six hundred twenty five milligrams of a hallucinogen." He argued that because of the statute's specific language, the prosecutor was required to prove not only that Ryan knew the mushrooms contained psilocybin, but also that he knew they contained at least 625 mgs of the substance.

Knowledge of Weight

THE COURT OF APPEAL rejected Mr. Ryan's argument, holding that knowledge of *the amount of* pure psilocybin contained in the mushroom was *not* an element of the crime. The prosecutor, said the court, must simply prove that a defendant knew the mushrooms contained psilocybin, and that the actual weight of the psilocybin itself, regardless of whether the defendant knew it, was at least 625 mgs.

In Mr. Ryan's case, explained the court of appeal, the prosecutor had presented sufficient evidence showing that Mr. Ryan knew the mushrooms contained psilocybin, as well as the testimony of a forensic scientist that a uniform sample of 140 grams of the mushrooms yielded well in excess of 625 milligrams of psilocybin. Accordingly, the court of appeal held that the prosecutor successfully proved his case. Mr. Ryan's indeterminate prison term of ten-years-to-life was upheld.

15

The Atley Case

THE IOWA SUPREME COURT ruled in early 1997 that a person who cultivates *Psilocybe* mushrooms knowing that they naturally produce the controlled substances psilocybin and psilocin, is guilty of "manufacturing" those substances. No extraction or attempt to extract, held the court, is required for a manufacturing conviction. [*State v. Atley* (Ia. 1997) 564 N.W.2d 817.]

The case began in the summer of 1994 when Davenport police received a telephone call from the Denver police who reported that they had intercepted a package containing methamphetamine, which would be arriving that afternoon at the Quad City airport. The call prompted officers to stakeout the airport, waiting for the package's recipient. Mr. Lewis Atley was the person who arrived to claim the package.

As Mr. Atley left the airport with the package, the officers secretly followed his vehicle into Iowa and then pulled him over on the interstate. In the emotional heat of the roadside detention, Mr. Atley gave the police consent to search his home, telling them that they would find a small amount of marijuana there and something else that would "make front page news."

In Mr. Atley's home the officers found a large mushroom-growing operation. Inside were over 4000 mason jars, 2000 Styrofoam coolers, 240 petri dishes, four 50-pound bags of brown rice, and numerous other tools of mushroom cultivation, including refrigerators, humidifiers, grow lights, pressure cookers, heat sealers, and packaging materials.

Mr. Atley told the officers that he was growing many species of mushrooms, and that he did not believe that mushroom cultivation was a crime. He admitted selling some of the mushrooms for $800 per pound.

When the police told him that the mushrooms were illegal "hallucinogens," Mr. Atley agreed to act as an informant, thereby convincing the police not to take him into custody. The next day, however, Mr. Atley could not be found.

With Mr. Atley gone, the police continued their investigation by searching Mr. Atley's home a second time, now armed with a search warrant. They also searched several post office boxes rented in Mr. Atley's name. These searches uncovered what officers said were proceeds and property derived from Atley's sale of "hallucinogenic" mushrooms. A random sampling of the Mason jars and petri dishes found in Mr. Atley's home tested positive for the controlled substance psilocybin. The officers then destroyed all the untested mushrooms and mycelia.

Four months later, agents located and arrested Mr. Atley in Florida. He was extradited to Iowa where, among other charges, he was tried for "manufacturing psilocybin," and for "possession of psilocybin with intent to deliver." A jury found him guilty as charged and he appealed.

Destruction of Evidence

IN THE ATLEY CASE, as in many mushroom cases, the prosecution only took random samples of the seized mushrooms and mycelia. Judges in drug cases have routinely upheld such random testing and destruction of untested samples. Atley, however, claimed, from the very first day, that only a portion of the mushrooms found growing in his home were entheogenic. The rest, he said, were medicinal and gourmet. By destroying the untested mushrooms, the government unfairly prevented Atley from introducing evidence to this effect.

Under Iowa law, psilocybin is a controlled substance. The same section also declares that "any material, compound, mixture, or preparation, which contains any quantity of [psilocybin]" is itself a controlled substance. Another section makes it a felony to "manufacture, deliver, or possess with the intent to manufacture or deliver, a controlled substance."

Inadequate Notice

Mr. Atley argued that the sections, even when read in combination, failed to give him—or any other person—adequate notice that the cultivation of a particular species of *mushroom* was a crime and that, therefore, his conviction violated the United States Constitution's guarantee to due process of law. He admitted cultivating the mushrooms found in his home, but argued that the act of growing mushrooms that endogenously contain psilocybin could not be equated with "manufacturing" psilocybin without some evidence that he extracted or attempted to extract that substance from the mushrooms.

To declare him to be "manufacturing" psilocybin simply by growing mushrooms that naturally produce that chemical would mean, by the government's logic, that thousands of gardeners who grow common varieties of morning glories are, in fact, criminals "manufacturing" lysergic acid amide (aka LA-111), a Schedule III controlled substance under federal law.

Unconstitutionally Vague

MR. ATLEY FURTHER ARGUED that when the Iowa Legislature intends to make a *specific plant* illegal to grow, it lists *the plant* by name as controlled, independent of separate provisions scheduling *a substance* that could be extracted from the plant.

Under Iowa law, for example, the plants *Cannabis sativa* and *Lophophora williamsii* are both explicitly scheduled even though their respective psychoactive constituents tetrahydrocannabinol (THC) and mescaline, are *also* scheduled. For these reasons, Mr. Atley argued that Iowa's anti-drug laws were unconstitutionally vague if they were said to apply to unnamed, unscheduled plants or mushrooms.

Court Decision

THE IOWA SUPREME COURT rejected Mr. Atley's arguments and affirmed his convictions. The court acknowledged that mushrooms were not explicitly listed in the state's schedule of controlled substances. Nevertheless, the Legislature had outlawed any "material" that contains psilocybin. *Mushrooms*, said the court, were "materials:"

> The legislature's use of the phrase "any material...which contains...psilocybin"...eads us to the conclusion that *[P]silocybe* mushrooms fall within the proscribed category of hallucinogens, regardless of whether Atley was actually engaged in extracting the psilocybin from them. Certainly a *[P]silocybe* mushroom is a "material containing psilocybin," under the ordinary and reasonable use of these words....

Having declared that mushrooms were within the statute's meaning of "material," the court–perhaps tacitly recognizing that Mr. Atley's void for vagueness argument had merit–opted to dodge the issue entirely by holding that *Mr. Atley* could not raise the issue *in the abstract*.

Vague as Applied

"A DEFENDANT," wrote the court, "charged with the violation of a statute has standing to claim the statute is unconstitutionally vague *as applied to him or her*...[but] does not necessarily have standing to claim, in addition, that a statute is unconstitutional as applied to others. If a statute is constitutional as applied to the defendant, the defendant lacks standing to make a facial challenge unless a recognized exception applies."

Given the large scale of Mr. Atley's mushroom growing operation, his admission that he sold the mushrooms for as much as $800 per pound, the fact that he used several aliases, and the fact that he had a previous arrest for mushroom cultivation, the appellate court was not persuaded that Atley was unaware that his conduct was illegal:

> Regardless of whether ambiguity may exist in other factual contexts (such as when a person unknowingly gathers *[P]silocybe* mushrooms in the wild), Atley was fairly apprised of the illegality of his conduct. The record strongly supports a determination that Atley had the necessary criminal knowledge and intent to possess and manufacture mushrooms containing psilocybin. He maintained an enormous growing operation, constituting the majority of space in his residence. He told an officer that he sold the mushrooms for $800 per pound, had numerous aliases and used different post office boxes to facilitate his trade. He professed to be an expert on mushroom cultivation and the law governing it. Atley had also been the subject of previous criminal proceedings for possession and manufacturing of *[P]silocybe* mushrooms in another jurisdiction.
>
> Based on these facts, Atley can hardly claim that his conduct was innocent and that he ignorantly

> violated the statute. We do not believe that a person of ordinary intelligence would not be able to determine that knowingly cultivating and selling hallucinogenic mushrooms would fall within the purview of the statute.

Atley's Previous Arrest

IN AN EARLIER CASE in Colorado involving Mr. Atley an apartment manager, acting on a neighbor's call of a water leak, used a pass-key to enter an apartment rented by Atley's girlfriend. The apartment manager was struck by the apartment's cold, humid, and musty environment. Poking around inside, the manager found that apart from a small black-and-white television set and a single chair, there was no furniture, no clothes, no food, and no other signs of residential use.

The apartment manager observed fifteen styrofoam coolers lined with tinfoil on the apartment floor. Inside the coolers she saw objects covered by what she later told police was "a mold-type substance." She also saw approximately twenty cases of canning jars and three or four coolers containing soil. The air conditioner in the apartment was operating at full capacity during the month of March and a humidifier was blowing. Three ultraviolet grow lights were in the apartment and one was in use. These discoveries led to the issuance of a search warrant, and to Atley's arrest and prosecution in Colorado. [*People v. Atley* (Colo. 1986) 727 P.2d 376.]

No Knowledge

IN A SEPARATE SENTENCE of its opinion, the court noted that a hypothetical person who cultivated or possessed *Psilocybe* mushrooms *without knowing that they contained the controlled substance psilocybin*, would escape conviction, because a prosecutor in a drug case must prove that the defendant knew that what he or she possessed was, or contained, a controlled substance. This requirement explained the court, "ensures that a person who innocently possesses *Psilocybe* mushrooms could not be successfully prosecuted under the [Iowa] statute because he or she would lack the necessary criminal intent."

While this is a very important protection, Mr. Atley clearly did not fall within this rule because he admitted knowing that some of the mushrooms he was growing did indeed produce the controlled substance psilocybin.

To the extent that the Iowa court recognized a person's lack of knowledge as a defense to a mushroom crime, it cannot be faulted. No one would argue that a person who has no idea that a plant or mushroom naturally produces a controlled substance should be unwittingly guilty of possessing the controlled substance simply by growing or possessing the plant. A different rule would require every person to become an expert mycologist just to remain on the right side of the law. As the Washington Supreme Court acknowledged in a 1979 drug case, "without the mental element of knowledge, even a postal carrier would be guilty of the crime were he innocently to deliver a package which in fact contained a forbidden narcotic."

Thought Crime

Unfortunately, after recognizing a "no-knowledge defense," the Iowa Supreme Court rashly and erroneously assumed that the corollary must be that someone who *does* know that a species of mushroom naturally produces a controlled substance is a criminal if he or she cultivates or possesses a mushroom of that species—even without any evidence that they have extracted or attempted to extract that controlled substance. The obvious problem with this rule, as stressed earlier, is that it makes criminal versus non-criminal status turn on a person's inner thoughts or knowledge!

It could have come from George Orwell's *Nineteen Eighty Four*:

> "*What are you in for?*" said Winston.
>
> "*Thought crime!*" said Parsons almost blubbering. The tone of his voice implied at once a complete admission of his guilt and a sort of incredulous horror that such a word could be applied to himself.
>
> He paused opposite Winston and began eagerly appealing to him: "*You don't think they'll shoot me, do you, old chap? They don't shoot you if you haven't actually done anything—only thoughts which you can't help? I know they give you a fair hearing. Oh, I trust them for that! They'll know my record, won't they? You know what kind of a chap I was. Not a bad chap in my way. Not brainy, of course, but keen. I tried to do my best for the Party, didn't I? I'll get off with five years, don't you think? Or even ten years? A chap like me could make himself pretty useful in a labor camp. They wouldn't shoot me for going off the rails just once?*"

Fairness

THE ONLY RULE THAT IS FAIR to gardeners and enforceable without "thought police" is the obvious one: the cultivation and possession of any plant or fungus should be legal so long as *the plant or fungus* has not been explicitly declared illegal by the legislature. (Assuming arguendo that a government of humans has the authority to outlaw other life forms, an assumption that is certainly open to argument.) To support a conviction for manufacturing psilocybin or psilocin – based on mushrooms – courts should require some evidence of extraction. Such logical and clear-cut rules would unambiguously put people on notice as to what plants and mushrooms may not be possessed or grown, and thereby draw a bright–and enforceable–line separating legal conduct from criminal conduct.

16

Canadian Cases

CANADIAN COURTS have generally distinguished mushrooms from their endogenous substances. For example, in *Regina v. Parnell* (1979, 51 Can.Crim.Cas.2d 413) convictions under Ca.Rev.Stat. 1970, ch. F-27, for possessing mushrooms containing psilocybin, were reversed by the B.C. Court of Appeal, which held that the statute could not be construed as prohibiting possession of mushrooms since it made no mention of mushrooms. [Accord. *Regina v. Cartier* (1980) 13 Alta.2d 164, 54 Can.Crim.Cas.2d 32; Re Coutu and Prieur and the Queen (1981) 61 Can.Crim.Cas.2d 149.]

In *Parnell*, the defendant argued that a conviction for possession of the controlled substance psilocybin cannot be based on possession of a mushroom that naturally produces psilocybin. Justice Nemetz, the Chief Justice of British Columbia, agreed, stating "...to sustain a charge of [drug] possession in a case such as this, evidence would have to be adduced, and the Crown prove beyond a reasonable doubt, that the person charged possessed psilocybin in a form other than that in which it occurs freely in nature."

In *Cartier*, Chief Justice McGillivray of Alberta, relied upon the *Parnell* case, holding that *Psilocybe* mushrooms do not fall within the definition of "restricted drug." Justice McGillivray reasoned that when the Canadian Parliament used the term "restricted drug" the legislature did not intend to prohibit the possession of materials in their natural state, but was aiming at drugs which would ordinarily be manufactured commercially.

Part III

Defenses

17

Substance Versus Mushroom Defense

AS THE CASES in the previous chapters show, while the law is relatively clear concerning the *substances* psilocybin and psilocin, it is exceedingly vague with regard to *mushrooms* that endogenously produce those substances. With the exception of California, neither the states nor the federal government have enacted laws that expressly schedule or otherwise control mushrooms that naturally produce the substances psilocybin or psilocin.

This substance-versus-mushroom issue provides the groundwork theory for a possible defense to mushroom charges. Under this defense, the fungophile argues that his or her possession of a mushroom is not a crime, because state statutes do not declare mushrooms (of any kind) to be controlled substances. The following sections will discuss aspects of this defense.

Mixtures or Materials

UNDER THE CSA, "any material, compound, mixture, or preparation, which contains any quantity of [psilocybin or psilocin], or which contains any of their salts, isomers, or salts of isomers" is also considered a Schedule I controlled substance. Prosecutors often argue that *Psilocybe* mushrooms are illegal mixtures, "compounds mixtures, or preparations" that contain psilocybin and psilocin.

Cutting Agents

THESE "MIXTURES" PROVISIONS were designed to penalize street level drug dealers who stretch their profits by diluting drugs such as cocaine and methamphetamine. Also, many illicit drugs—like licit drugs—are manufactured in tablet form and, hence, contain only a percentage of the pure drug. The balance of the tablet is inert binding compounds and perhaps some adulterants or diluents.

Under the "mixture," "material," or "container" provisions, prosecutors were excused from the time and expense associated with having to tediously. separate legal cutting agents, binders and diluents from the pure illegal drug before determining how much of the illegal substance the defendant possessed.

In other words, a person convicted of distributing a baggie of methamphetamine diluted with a cutting agent such as Vita-blend, will have his or her punishment calculated based on the *entire* weight of the "mixture" although, say, thirty percent of the gross weight may be the innocuous cutting agent.

The correct application of the "material," "mixture," or "container" provision can be found in *U.S. v. Crowell*, where defendants in Arizona were convicted of conspiring to distribute dilaudid tablets. The defendants' sentences were calculated based on the *entire* weight of the dilaudid *tablets*, rather than just the weight of the controlled substance (hydromorphine) contained in the tablets. The *Crowell* case shows the correct application of the "mixture," "material" or "container" provision. The provision was *not* designed to encompass whole unprocessed life forms–such as mushrooms, nor would any reasonable person so interpret it. [*U.S. v. Crowell* (Ariz. 1993) 9 F.3d 1452; see also, *U.S. v. Shabazz* (1991) 933 F.2d 1029.]

Reductionist Definitions

THE AVERAGE PERSON would not ordinarily think of mushrooms as "containers," "mixtures," or "materials." It is certainly not within the ordinary use of the noun "material," to greet a mushroom hunter at the end of an early morning foray by saying: "Those are some nice looking *materials* you have there in your basket." Nor would anyone exclaim the morning after a fall rain, "my yard is filled with *containers* that popped up over night!"

In fact, researchers Christian in 1977 and Callaway in 1995 pointed out that such extreme reductionist definitions that equate life forms with "containers" or "mixtures," would make possession of our own brains a crime for the simple reason that the illegal "hallucinogen" dimethyltryptamine (DMT) is naturally found in cerebrospinal fluid.

Outlawing Nature

INDEED, a host of controlled substances are ubiquitous in nature. DMT, for example, is so common that a chapter in the book *TIHKAL*, by Alexander Shulgin, Ph.D., an expert entheogen chemist, is titled "DMT is Everywhere." Similarly, the controlled substance lysergic acid amide–aka LA-111–one possible precursor to LSD that is psychoactive in its own right–is found in the seeds of common varieties of morning glories available at nearly any garden store. *Pharmacotheon* by Ott, lists over 250 plants known (thus far) to endogenously produce scheduled entheogens.

The controlled substance mescaline is found in numerous species of cacti, some of which can be found in the garden centers of national hardware chains, though peyote (*Lophophora williamsii*) is the only cactus outlawed by the federal government. Add to this list, the unscheduled plants that naturally contain various opiates and numerous other controlled substances, and suddenly a great deal of the natural world would be off-limits under the mushrooms-are-mixtures theory.

Specific Plants

FURTHERMORE, a reading of the state and federal drug laws indicates that when the government has intended to outlaw the possession of *specific plants*, it has done so by explicitly naming the *plant*. For example, the government has not only outlawed possession of the *substances* cocaine, THC, opium, ibogaine, and mescaline, but it has also, by naming the specific source *plants* themselves, outlawed possession of coca leaves, all plants of the genus *Cannabis*, opium poppies (*Papaver somniferum*), *Tabernantha iboga*, which is the primary natural source of ibogaine, and *Lophophora williamsii*—the mescaline-rich *peyote* cactus. The corollary is, or logically should be, that those plant sources of drugs that are *not listed* as scheduled substances are *not* controlled.

Yet, because the various criminal laws refer only to the *substances*, psilocybin and psilocin, and say nothing about mushrooms, prosecutors have argued that *Psilocybe* mushrooms are "mixtures," "materials," or "containers" of psilocybin and psilocin and that the mushrooms themselves are outlawed substances whenever possessed or cultivated by someone who knows they naturally produce psilocybin and psilocin.

Criminal Absurdity

SHOULDN'T THE GOVERNMENT draw the line between criminality and non-criminality by reference to a person's *action*—such as extracting a controlled substance from a plant—rather by reference to a person's inner thoughts or phytochemical knowledge? As a basic axiom of justice, the government has an obligation to draw a *clear* line separating non-criminal conduct from criminal conduct. Basing criminal status on whether or not a person knows the chemistry of various plants and mushrooms is inviting all sorts of inequities and enforcement problems, to say nothing of its astonishingly Orwellian character.

Simply put, the argument that mushrooms fall within the meaning of "material," "mixture," or "container," is not only illogical within the context of other anti-drug laws, but downright absurd. Nevertheless, the *vast majority* of psilocybin and psilocin arrests are premised *on mushrooms* containing those substances. And, because most defense attorneys have never stopped to think about the substance-versus-mushroom issue, it is very seldom raised as a defense. Consequently, the consensus has developed that "shrooms" are unquestionably illegal. With that consensus now in place, it is no easy task to win the substance-versus-mushroom argument in a court of law.

Any police officer who finds a person in possession of psilocybian mushrooms will likely arrest the person. Likewise, since most attorneys are unaware of the substance-versus-mushroom issue, the defendants in most mushroom cases plead guilty never raising the argument. As a result, most players in the "criminal justice system" have come to presume, without examination, that *Psilocybe* mushrooms are illegal. Consequently, unless a person is prepared to actively fight his or her case, and able to find and afford an attorney who understands the issue, the person is wise to assume that "in the eyes of the law," mushrooms which endogenously produce psilocybin or psilocin are illegal to possess, grow, or distribute.

Yet, there remains no reported *federal* decision on the issue of mushrooms versus substances, and only eight *state* court's–i.e., Florida, Illinois, Indiana, Iowa, Kansas, New York, Ohio, and Washington–have published opinions on the issue as discussed in previous chapters. Six of these courts have held that possession of *mushrooms* by someone who knows that they naturally produce psilocybin or psilocin is unlawful. Florida and Ohio cases have held otherwise.

18

Religious Defense

INGESTING ENTHEOGENIC MUSHROOMS is unquestionably a primary religious experience for many people. Anyone who eats over four grams of the dried mushrooms can verify first-hand that the mushrooms have the potential to release one into the *unio mystica*, the source of being and nonbeing. Indeed, McKenna reported that evidence of the religious use of sacred mushrooms dates back to Paleolithic times.

Under the Free Exercise Clause of the First Amendment to the U.S. Constitution, religious freedom is "guaranteed" a very high level of protection against government coercion. The Free Exercise Clause, however, is interpreted and applied by judges, and to-date not a single person has succeeded at arguing that his or her use or cultivation of sacred mushrooms is protected religious activity.

No Free Exercise Protection

THE U.S. SUPREME COURT eviscerated the Free Exercise Clause in 1990, holding that the Free Exercise Clause of the First Amendment did not block the state of Oregon from making peyote a controlled substance and outlawing *all* peyote use - including religious use. While this astonishingly unjust decision did not involve mushrooms, the parallels between mushrooms and peyote are obvious.

Religious Freedom Restoration Act (RFRA)

The Religious Freedom Restoration Act of 1993 (42 U.S.C.A. Section 2000bb) was designed by Congress to protect the free exercise of religion. RFRA states, in part:

> [T]he government shall not substantially burden a persons exercise of religion even if the burden results from the rule of general applicability person whose religious exercise has been substantially burdened in violation of this section may assert that violation as a claim or defense in a judicial proceeding.

Pursuant to RFRA, the U.S. government must accommodate a person's religious conduct unless there is a compelling government interest that all but makes accommodation impossible. The government has the burden of proving such an overriding interest once a defendant shows that a law substantially burdens his or her religious practice.

In 1997, the U.S. Supreme Court ruled that RFRA was unconstitutional because it improperly infringed upon the states' rights to control their own police power. (See *City of Boerne v. Flores* (1997) 521 U.S. 507.) As a result, RFRA provides no help for persons seeking to present a defense to state drug charges. There remains, however, a glimmer of hope that RFRA retains some validity in federal court.

The U.S. Court of Appeals for the Ninth Circuit has ruled that some marijuana-using Rastafarians *might* be protected under RFRA. [*Guam v. Guerrero* (9th Cir. 2002) No. 00-71247.]

The case began in 1991 when Benny Guerrero, returning from a trip to Hawaii, was stopped by officials at Guam's international airport. Mr. Guerrero evidently attracted the eyes of authority because he was carrying a book about Rastafarianism and marijuana. A search of Guerrero's luggage turned up five ounces of marijuana and some Cannabis seeds. He was arrested and charged with importation of a controlled substance.

In his defense, Guerrero argued that he was a practicing Rastafarian and that his use of marijuana was religious.[1] His importation of the herb was, he argued, protected under RFRA.

After litigating the case for more than ten years, the Ninth Circuit ruled in 2002 that while RFRA might protect some Rastafarians who *possess or smoke* marijuana as part of their religious practices, it does *not* protect the *importation* of marijuana, even if that marijuana was intended for religious use. According to the Ninth Circuit, while the practice of

Rastafarianism sanctions the smoking of marijuana, nowhere does the religion sanction the *importation* of marijuana.

As Guerrero's lawyer pointed out, the Ninth Curcuit's ruling was "equivalent to saying wine is a necessary sacrament for some Christians but you have to grow your own grapes."

According to the latest Household Survey on Drug Abuse, over 16 million Americans used an illegal drug in the last 30 days. The overwhelming majority of these people, just like the overwhelming majority of people who use legal drugs, did so responsibly and without problems. Some of those people may find that their use of an illegal drug occasioned a religious experience, and others may find that use of an illegal drug provided pain relief that they have been unable to achieve by any other means. To the extent that the vast majority of these 16 million Americans used an illegal drug without causing harm to others, our criminal justice system ought to leave them alone and instead focus on protecting us from dangerous criminals.

Instead, the government continues to spend tens of billions of tax-payer dollars to fight yet another year of the "war on drugs" and it's not about to let religion, medicine, or basic human rights, for that matter, stand in its way.

Lost in the haze of its zero-tolerance prohibition policy, and drunk on its hyperbolic rhetoric about how drugs like marijuana and mushrooms lead you through the Devil's gateway, the government continues to flex its weary muscles in an antiquated effort to save as many souls from damnation as possible.

Part IV

Political Implications

19

Taxonomy

MOST—BUT NOT ALL—MUSHROOMS that naturally produce the entheogenic substances psilocybin and psilocin are found within the genus *Psilocybe*. However, not all species of mushrooms within the genus *Psilocybe* are psychoactive.

In the early 2000s information had been circulating that there may be a significant change in the way psilocybian mushrooms are classified by the International Code of Botanical Nomenclature (ICBN), the official system of nomenclature used by botanists in all countries. In addition to establishing the names of plants, the ICBN covers fungi. Rumor has it that the current taxonomy may be revised to create a new genus that will contain only those—formerly— *Psilocybe* mushrooms that are indeed psychoactive. In other words, if the change occurs, the genus known as "*Psilocybe*" will contain *only non-psychoactive* mushroom species, and the new genus will contain only *psychoactive* species that can produce psilocybin or psilocin.

The preamble to the ICBN notes the importance of maintaining stable, or unchanging, nomenclature, and states that changes to established plant or fungi names are disfavored. "The only proper reasons for changing a name," states the ICBN "are either a more profound knowledge of the facts resulting from adequate taxonomic study or the necessity of giving up a nomenclature that is contrary to the rules." It is not entirely clear what new "profound knowledge" about Psilocybes may now exist, or whether the existing nomenclature for *Psilocybe* is "contrary to the rules." The proposed change is based on DNA analyses that may have pinpointed a genetic difference between *Psilocybe* species that can produce psilocybin or psilocin and those that do not. From the law and freedom perspective, such a change in nomenclature presents some problems.

At the present moment no federal or state law—except California's and Georgia's—specifically outlaws mushrooms of the genus *Psilocybe*. Instead the laws all proscribe the active principles psilocybin and psilocin. As a result, when the authorities want to prosecute a mushroom case, the prosecutors argue that any mushroom psilocybin or psilocin is an illegal "mixture" or "material" containing a controlled substance. Thus, when a person is arrested in possession of a *Psilocybe* mushroom, the prosecutor—if challenged by a savvy defense attorney—is not only required to factually establish that the mushroom actually contains a controlled substance, but he or she must also establish that such a mushroom falls within the meaning of the words "mixture" or "material" as those terms are used in the controlled substance laws. This is a pretty significant burden on a prosecutor, and can lead to a defendant's acquittal.

May Spur Scheduling

CREATING A NEW GENUS that contains only psilocybin- or psilocin-producing mushrooms may spur legislation expressly scheduling any mushroom in that genus. The new genus would provide legislators with a tidy and targetable category, which they could easily add to the list of scheduled substances. Were this to occur, all the existing obstacles that stand in the way of a mushroom prosecution would be removed. Rather than require a prosecutor to prove that a mushroom actually contains psilocybin or psilocin and that it is properly considered a "mixture" or "material," the new nomenclature would only require a prosecutor to prove the identity of the mushroom as one contained within the newly scheduled genus.

Further, if a new psilocybin-producing genus is created, and if it does spur scheduling legislation, the new legislation will likely also outlaw "spores" of the new genus, which do not, themselves, contain any controlled substances. This is discussed more fully in the section on mushroom spores and mushroom growing kits which follows. This would be analogous to current law with regard to *Cannabis* plants. State and federal laws proscribe viable *Cannabis* seeds, even though they contain no appreciable THC.

Matters could be made even worse if the new taxonomic name gives an overt nod to the fact that the mushrooms are psychoactive. For example, at one point a reliable source mentioned that one name being considered for the new genus was "*Psychedelia*." While this name no longer appears to be under consideration, a similar name could paint a prominent bull's eye on the new genus prompting legislators to outlaw it.

20

Legal Harm Reduction

The purpose of the material presented in this chapter is to help you to better understand yourself and a few of your important constitutional rights. This information is not legal advice nor should not be considered as encouragement to violate the state or federal controlled substance laws.

SACRED MUSHROOM USERS in the 21st Century are on unsettled legal ground. As we've seen, only a few states have laws or court cases that directly address the legal status of psychoactive mushrooms. Nevertheless, the predominant mindset among police officers and prosecutors is that all psychoactive mushrooms are illegal. As a result, those who are found growing, picking, selling or cultivating psychoactive mushrooms will almost always be arrested, and forced to present their defense in court.

Your Risk Aversion Level

GIVEN THAT THE LAW concerning psychoactive mushrooms is unsettled and mostly hostile, a person with an interest in sacred mushrooms should maintain a respect for the dangerous legal terrain underfoot and act with the appropriate degree of awareness and caution.

An aficionado of sacred mushrooms might want to candidly consider his or her own level of legal risk aversion. This is often a difficult analysis to make. As a simple guide to determining risk aversion, two considerations are important: the impact on your life of being *arrested* for a drug crime and the impact on your life for being *convicted* of such a crime.

Levels of Risk

BEING "ARRESTED" MEANS the police take you into custody, and you spend anywhere from a few hours in jail to several days—maybe several weeks if you're denied bail and have to remain in custody pending a trial—but you eventually win your case and escape a criminal conviction. Even so, simply being arrested and held in jail could have a dramatic impact on your life.

By contrast, being "convicted" means actually being arrested, *and* convicted of a criminal drug offense. If convicted, you will likely be imprisonment as well as fined. You might have to do community service. It is likely that you will be monitored for several years by government parole or probation agents. This could have a life-changing impact on your life and the lives of your family.

These are important considerations that the wise consider before embarking upon the dangerous course of experimenting with sacred mushrooms.

Anyone with an active interest in sacred mushrooms should take some time to collect his or her thoughts on these issues, undertake an individualized assessment of one's own level of risk aversion, and live with a level of awareness and caution in accordance with that evaluation. The following risk tolerance quiz can help start the assessment process.

What Is Your Risk Tolerance Level?

Using a scale from 1 to 5, where 1 is very unlikely and 5 is highly likely, rate how likely each of the following eventualities would be if you were arrested and if you were convicted of a drug crime.

If I were arrested for a drug crime:

__ I would be humiliated.
__ My family would be ridiculed.
__ My friends and family would think negatively of me.
__ I would be excluded from social circles I care about.
__ I would lose my job and/or a professional license.
__ I could not afford a top-notch lawyer.
__ I would not be able to pay bail.

IF I WERE CONVICTED OF A DRUG CRIME:

__ I would be humiliated.
__ My family would be ridiculed.
__ People I care about would think negatively of me.
__ I would be excluded from social circles I care about.
__ I would lose my job and/or a professional license.
__ I would not have enough funds to make a legal appeal.
__ Incarceration would seriously disrupt my life.

SCORING:

14 - 20 **Risk Neutral**
You can probably withstand both an arrest and a criminal conviction.

21 - 30 **Moderately Risk Aversive**
You could probably withstand an arrest so long as you were ultimately acquitted.

31 - 70 **Highly Risk Aversive**
Merely being *arrested* would take an unacceptable toll on your life as currently lived.

Do not take your "score" too seriously–it is not scientific. The point of the quiz is to stop and really consider what could happen you were arrested and possibly convicted of a criminal drug crime is to for you to pause and realistically take an account of your situation. It's also presented to emphasize the very important difference between avoiding *conviction* versus avoiding *arrest*. For many people, suffering an arrest, even if they ultimately avoid conviction, would be enough to bring their world crashing down.

You Must Consent to a Search

BECAUSE THE USE, cultivation, or purchase of mushrooms are all victimless crimes, police officers have a fairly difficult time learning about such behavior. The result is that the *overwhelming* number of mushroom-related arrests occur as the direct result of a serendipitous discovery made by a police officer while investigating a non-mushroom related offense.

For example, many people have been arrested after a police officer stopped their vehicle for a minor traffic infraction and found mushrooms in the car after the driver foolishly consented to a search. A sizeable number of arrests have also occurred after police responded to a loud party and saw mushrooms or evidence of their use in plain view.

It's very common for police officers to use a minor offense or infraction to go on a fishing trip for drugs. A common occurrence is when a police officer stops a motorist for a minor vehicle code violation, such as a broken brake light, and has a hunch that the occupants might be in possession of drugs. In such circumstances, it's extremely common for the police officer to "ask" the motorist to consent to a search of the automobile.

You Can Refuse

GRANTING CONSENT to an officer's request to search has been, in many cases, the action that led directly to the arrest of a visionary plant or fungi aficionado–an arrest which would not have occurred had the person simply refused to consent. Under the Fourth Amendment you always have a right to refuse to grant consent to a police officer's request to search you, your car, your home, or your belongings.

Some police officers are forthright and plainly ask for consent to search the car for drugs. Many other officers, however, are not so forthright and will sneakily phrase their request to make it easily misinterpreted as *requiring* compliance. For example, after handling the routines of the traffic violation the officer might ask the driver, "Would you please step out of the car and open the trunk of your car?" While the written version of this request ends in a question mark, when spoken out-loud by a police officer it is not nearly so apparent that the officer is making a request and not ordering the driver to open the trunk.

Under the Fourth Amendment you always have a right to refuse to grant consent to a police officer's request to search you, your car, your home, or your belongings.

When faced with a police officer who is making a stern request, many people understandably become nervous and mistakenly believe that they must comply with the officer's request. Yet, the truth is just the opposite, under the Fourth Amendment you have a right to refuse consent everytime a police officer is asking for your consent to search. Such a request by a police office is equivalent to asking you to waive your rights under the Fourth Amendment–something you should never do without a lawyer being present.

To help ease the awkwardness that many people feel when standing-up to a police officer, some people have told the officer that they're late for an important appointment and need to be on their way. Other people have been able to redirect some of the stress, by telling the officer that their company lawyer has advised employees never to consent to a warrantless search and that he or she is just following the lawyer's advice. However, the bottom line–which bears repeating–is that a person should never consent to a search or waive any other constitutional protection unless they are doing so after consulting with a criminal defense attorney.

Cannot Be Held Against You

REFUSING TO CONSENT cannot be used against you. Some people erroneously think that the very act of refusing to let an officer conduct a consensual search would in itself give the officer probable cause to believe that one is in possession of contraband. This might make commonsense on first blush. However, there is a very good reason why such a presumption by police officers is not permitted under the law. It would effectively destroy the Fourth Amendment by turning it into a "tails you lose; heads the officer wins" double bind. regardless of whether the person granted consent or with held consent, the officer would be permitted to search and thereby make an end-run around the Fourth Amendment simply by prefacing any warrantless search with a request for consent. For this reason, the United States Supreme Court has made very clear that *a person's*

Never waive your constitutional rights without legal advice.

refusal to consent may not itself be used by police officers to justify a warrantless search.

Refusing to consent to an officer's warrantless search is, at bottom, simply a means of protecting one's privacy. Unless one is a risk neutral "activist" who relishes the opportunity to get arrested in order to present some sort of gallant defense to right the wrongs of the anti-drug laws, it's a good idea to take advantage of all the constitutional guarantees protecting one's privacy.

Keep Private Items Private

MANY CASES TEACH that in addition to refusing to consent to a search, mushroom aficionados should always keep dried mushrooms out of view. Remember, police officers are neither mushroom experts nor legal experts, and a baggie of dried mushrooms of any kind could be enough to trigger an arrest.

Closed–better yet, locked–opaque containers receive a high degree of privacy protections. Briefcases, perhaps because many judges use them to carry their own private items, have been recognized as particularly private containers. One federal court described this particular characteristic of briefcases, noting:

> A briefcase is often the repository for more than business documents. Rather, it is the extension of one's own clothing because it serves as a larger "pocket" in which such items as wallets and credit cards, address books, personal calendar/diaries, correspondence, and reading glasses often are carried. *Few places outside one's home justify a greater expectation of privacy than does the briefcase.* (United States v. Ramos (11th Cir. 1996) 12 F.3d 1019, 1024.)

Festivals

AN EXCEPTION TO ARRESTS resulting from the serendipitous discovery of mushrooms arises when law enforcement agents identify a particular event which they believe will involve a large proportion of drug users–including mushroom users.

Many arrests occurred at Grateful Dead concerts for just this reason. Supporting this practice, a DEA agent said, "We go where the drugs happen to be–at the concerts." Each year, dozens of people are arrested at various outdoor events that used words like "weed," "hemp," or "marijuana" in the event name and promotions.

Normally, police officers and DEA agents are far more focused on "addictive" drugs or those with a much larger user base, like marijuana, than they are with the more esoteric shamanic inebriants. Police are, however, at least remotely familiar with psychoactive mushrooms and a significant number of people have been arrested for mushroom-related offenses at such events.

Mushrooms in the Mail

IT IS THEORIZED that the United States Post Office and private express mail services are the largest traffickers in scheduled substances–unwittingly, of course. With over 180 billion pieces of mail delivered each year–580 million per day, it is obviously impossible for the post office and private carriers to detect all the drugs sent through the mail. Nevertheless, each year, the post office and private mail carriers seize millions of dollars worth of scheduled substances, then make controlled deliveries of the letters or packages and arrest the recipient.

Some of these seizures have been the result of the package fitting the "drug package profile." A significant number of seizures have also been the result of a serendipitous discovery made when a package was poorly packaged, damaged in transit or found leaking a suspicious substance.

In some criminal cases, Federal Express employees have testified that it is the company's police to open and examine the contents of any packages that become damaged in transit. Employees have also testified that packages are routinely opened if Federal Express cannot resolve a delivery problem. In such cases, the company opens the package to see whether any useful delivery information can be found inside. As a nongovernmental entity, Federal Express does not need a search warrant to open packages sent via its service.

In contrast to private mail delivery companies, the US Postal Service–which is operated by the federal government–is constrained by the Constitution and, with a few exceptions, cannot open first-class mail without first obtaining a federal search warrant. Using the US Postal Service or a private carrier like Federal Express to send a package containing a controlled substance is a federal offense punishable by up to four years in federal prison and a $30,000 fine. (21 USC Sec. 843.)

Mushroom Extracts

UNDER FEDERAL LAW, and the laws of every state, it is considered "manufacturing" a controlled substance to extract a controlled substance from a plant or mushroom. Therefore, the extraction process alone can be a key turning point between an arguably lawful mushroom and an illegal controlled substance. Legally speaking, it is *much* safer to possess a mushroom that endogenously produces a scheduled substance then it is to possess an extract of that mushroom. While few people would naturally term a mushroom a "mixture," most people would consider an extract which contains psilocybin or psilocin to be a an illegal "mixture containing a controlled substance."

The extraction process alone can be a key turning point between an arguably lawful mushroom and an illegal controlled substance.

Conclusion

WE END AS WE BEGAN—forever circling and cycling round and round. Mushrooms confound the law, much like they confound all that is culture-bound, mechanistic, or fixed. The mushroom can be found only on the fringes of the law, in the shadows, off the beaten track. Seldom named, its identity always dangerously uncertain, the mushroom is all but invisible on the legal landscape—it leaves the law's compass spinning.

Those who venture onto such terrain and eat of its fruits know well the indescribable and paradoxical powers of these one-legged friends. My hope is that this book has provided some cartographic considerations for orienting on this strangley textured legal surface. I bid you good fortune on your journeys.

Bibliography

Arons, Stephen, and Charles Lawrence. "The Manipulation of Consciousness: A First Amendment Critique of Schooling" in *Harvard Civil Rights: Civil Liberties Law Review*, Fall 1980, 15(2), (312) pg. 309-361.

Callaway, Jace, et al. "Endogenous ß-Carbolines and Other Indole Alkaloids in Mammals," *Integration*, 5, 1995, pg. 19-33.

Christian, S., et al. "The in vitro identification of dimethyltryptamine (DMT) in the mammalian brain and its characterization as a possible endogenous neuroregulatory agent," 1977, *Biochemical Medicine*, 18, pg. 164-183.

McKenna, Terence, *Food of the Gods*, Bantam, New York, 1992.

Munn, Henry, "The Mushrooms of Language", *Hallucinogens and Shamanism*, ed. M. Harner, Oxford University Press, 1973, pg. 88-89.

Orwell, George, *Ninteen Eighty Four*, Martin Secker & Warburg, London, 1949.

Ott, Jonathan, *Pharmacotheon: Entheogenic Drugs, Their Plant Sources and History*, 2nd Ed., Natonal Products Co., Kennewick, WA, 1997.

Ruck, Carl, et al., "Entheogens," in *Journal of Psychedelic Drugs*, 1979, 11(1-2) 146.

Shulgin, Alexander & Ann Shulgin, *TIHKAL: The Continuation, Transform Press, Berkeley*, CA, *1997*.

Shulgin, Alexander, personal communication, September, 1997.

Stamets, Paul, *Psilocybin Mushrooms of the World*, Ten Speed Press, Berkeley, Ca, 1996.

Tribe, Lawrence. *American Constitutional Law*, Foundation Press, 1978.

Wasson, R. Gordon, *Soma: Divine Mushroom of Immortality*, Ethno-Mycological Studies, No. 1, Mouton, The Hague, Netherlands, 1968.

Wilson, Peter Lamborn. "Neurospace," in *21-C* , Gordon and Breach, 1996, (3)32.

Membership dues and donations are tax-deductible, and all members in the Society receive a one-year subscription to the *Journal of Cognitive Liberties.*

If you believe that the world needs an organization giving voice to the critical importance of cognitive liberty, please join us.

For more information, or to become a member online, visit us on the Web at:
www.alchemind.org, or call us toll free at
1-888-950-MIND (6463).

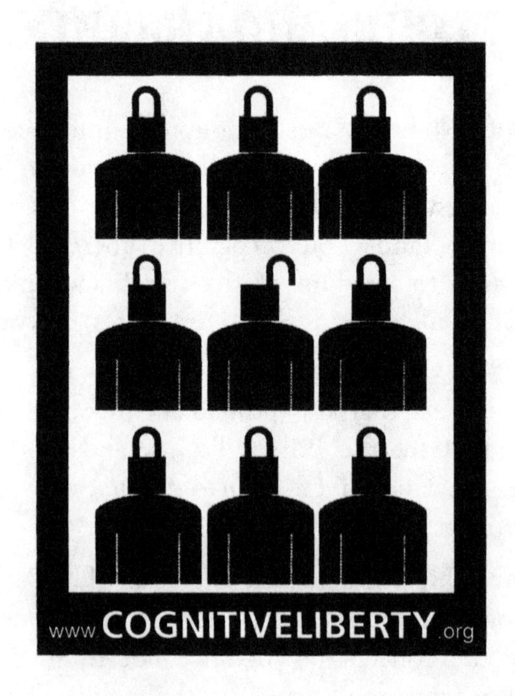

Printed in the USA
CPSIA information can be obtained
at www.ICGtesting.com
JSHW081746120224
57198JS00010B/1153